D1150922

JOHN DUNLOP was born in Newry, County Down, in 1939. He was educated at Newry Model School, the Royal Belfast Academical Institution and Newry Grammar School, studying later at Queen's University Belfast, New College in the University of Edinburgh and the Presbyterian Assembly's College in Belfast. He worked first in Belfast and then for ten years in Jamaica with the United Church of Jamaica and Grand Cayman. Since 1978 he has been the minister of Rosemary Presbyterian Church in north Belfast. In 1989 he was an Eisenhower Exchange Fellow in the USA and in 1992–93 was the Moderator of the General Assembly of the Presbyterian Church in Ireland. During this period he visited the USA with Cardinal Cahal Daly, Archbishop Robin James and the Methodist President Derek Ritchie. In 1993 he received a Cultural Traditions Award in recognition of his contribution to the debate on cultural diversity in Northern Ireland. He is a regular contributor to radio and television broadcasts and to the press, and in 1993 was appointed Presbyterian Religious Adviser to Ulster Television. He lives in Belfast and is married with a daughter and a son.

A
PRECARIOUS
BELONGING

PRESBYTERIANS
AND THE
CONFLICT IN IRELAND

JOHN DUNLOP

9/433524

THE
BLACKSTAFF
PRESS

First published in May 1995 by
The Blackstaff Press Limited
3 Galway Park, Dundonald, Belfast BT16 0AN, Northern Ireland

Reprinted June and November 1995

This book has received support from the Cultural Traditions
Programme of the Community Relations Council, which aims to
encourage acceptance and understanding of cultural diversity.

© John Dunlop, 1995
All rights reserved

Typeset by Paragon Typesetters, Queensferry, Clwyd

Printed in Ireland by ColourBooks Limited

A CIP catalogue record for this book
is available from the British Library

ISBN 0-85640-559-0

CONTENTS

ACKNOWLEDGEMENTS

Every preacher needs space which permits the interplay of theology and the life situations in which the preacher and the congregation are found. I have been fortunate to have been given such space in the congregations of Fitzroy Avenue, Belfast, the Mount Hermon and Webster Memorial Churches in Jamaica and, for the last seventeen years, Rosemary Presbyterian Church in north Belfast. Jamaica was the most exciting of places to preach, Belfast the most difficult. In the midst of so much trauma and seeing through a glass darkly, one preaches in faith, hoping that what is said is both responsible and faithful.

I would like to thank the Blackstaff Press which took the risk, in the first instance, when it invited me to do what had never occurred to me to do, which was to write this book; the staff have been supportive and helpful throughout the process. I also gratefully acknowledge the suggestions made by the Very Reverend Professor Finlay Holmes and Jonathan Bardon as I attempted to sketch complex historical processes in too few words. Professor Desmond Rea, Gemma Loughran, the Rev. Drs Bert Tosh and David Lapsley were kind enough to take the trouble to read and offer suggestions on early drafts. Their help does not mean that they agree with everything in the final product.

Over the last number of years I have been invited by many organisations and interviewers to join with others in exploring the territory on the interface between religion and politics. This was a constantly stimulating and learning experience. To do this in public involved risks and resulted in less peace of mind than I might have wanted. But that was as nothing to the physical danger in which thousands of courageous people have found themselves over the last twenty-five years.

I thank the kirk session of Rosemary Presbyterian Church for very generously granting me partial leave of absence to write this book and engage in some other enterprises on the interfaces mentioned above.

Lastly, I would thank my wife, Rosemary, and my family, who were too often neglected while I, like most ministers, was preoccupied with the needs of other people.

JOHN DUNLOP
MARCH, 1995

INTRODUCTION

The people of Northern Ireland, both Catholics and Protestants, have suffered from twenty-five years of violence. As I write this in January 1995, a cease-fire is in operation which we hope will develop into a permanent peace. Over 3,200 people have been killed and over 37,000 injured. The accumulated legacy of bereavement, injury, dislocation, destruction, anger and mistrust is incalculable. In January 1995 David Bolton, a social worker from Enniskillen who counsels bereaved people from both communities told the Forum for Peace and Reconciliation in Dublin:

> The violence visited upon individuals, families and local communities has been of a measure which is at times unspeakable. To name some of the offences against people is to give us some insight into their suffering and loss. The indiscriminate violence which overwhelms in an instance; the sense of betrayal when someone has been targeted; the murder at a person's front door in front of his children; the violence which is so awful that families cannot even view the remains; the disfigurement and disabling of people who still live with the scars, the memories and the pain. These and many other experiences speak to us of

unjustifiable events which are beneath the dignity and nobility of the human race.

The consequences of violence perpetrated and suffered by both communities will not go away overnight. These matters cannot be simply forgotten, as if nothing has happened.

While the horror has been appalling, had it not been for the forbearance of most of the people, the violence would have been much worse. The constant calls of those most affected for forgiveness or for no retaliation have had a profoundly moderating influence on the wider population. We can imagine what it might have been like had this strong element of restraint been missing or if calls for revenge had fuelled even greater outrage. The cease-fire has made possible the beginnings of a more inclusive political dialogue which was never going to happen while the violence continued. It may be possible to reach some form of compromise and political accommodation which will address the complexities of the issues we face.

The problems in Ireland have to do with people and not with territory. The simplistic mythology of the 'four green fields' or the uncomplicated political statement that 'Ulster is British' have to give way to the complex reality of five million people living in two political jurisdictions whose identities and self-understandings intersect and are significantly marked by diversity. Amongst these people lie the Presbyterians, living largely, but not exclusively, in Northern Ireland. The Presbyterian Church in Ireland is the second largest Christian Church, next to the Catholic Church, in Northern Ireland, and the third largest, after the Catholic and Anglican Churches, in the whole of Ireland. If the people of Ireland are to be understood, it is clearly necessary to understand the Presbyterians: who they are, where they are coming from and how they see themselves.

The resistance to a united Ireland lies primarily with the Protestants in Northern Ireland, who are mainly of a broadly unionist persuasion. That is not to say that they do not have

quite strong elements of Irishness in their identity. Their resistance to a united Ireland has been rooted in the conviction that
they would be overwhelmed in a society that has not, until
recently, been much interested in diversity. A great wedge of
these people are Presbyterians.

Many people in the Presbyterian Church in Ireland feel like
invisible people. It is as if they do not exist. I startled an
American participant at a peace conference in Derry when I told
her that there were Presbyterians in Ireland and that I was one
of them. She did not know that any such people existed.

Recently a television company from London did extensive
interviews with people in Derry, including interviews with
Church leaders. This came to the notice of the Clerk of the
Derry and Strabane Presbytery who enquired why he had never
been approached. The television crew replied that they thought
the Presbyterians were such a small community that they did
not matter; and this after twenty-five years of saturation
coverage of Northern Ireland. One can only conclude that there
has been saturation coverage of a portion of it and significant
parts of it have gone unnoticed. It is a humiliating experience for
people to be overlooked, misinterpreted or rendered voiceless.

It is possible to speak about the collective 'self-understanding'
of the broader Protestant community. Within that collective
'self-understanding', it is necessary to identify the particularity
of the Presbyterians, who have had a different historical experience from their neighbours.

On a lovely summer's day, from some parts of the Antrim
Coast Road, the coast of Scotland looks like a peninsula of
Ireland. From that perspective, Dundalk seems a long way
away, never mind Dublin and Cork. For very many Presbyterians, their contemporary east–west orientations are much
stronger than any running north and south. These include not
only the Church but family associations, daily newspapers and
radio and television. The ecclesiological and historical roots of
Irish Presbyterians lie across that narrow strip of water and go

through Glasgow and Edinburgh to Geneva and thence, through the pre-Reformation Church, to Jerusalem, to Jesus and to the apostles with their definitive affirmations about the significance of Christ. The Presbyterian Church in Ireland is the senior 'daughter' of the Church of Scotland. Its Moderator is given primacy of honour at meetings of the General Assembly of the Church of Scotland. It remains the custom for many Irish Presbyterian ministers to study in the theological faculties of the ancient Scottish universities.

Presbyterian Church order has been described as democracy run riot. There are so many checks and balances; so much consultation; so many networks of support and defence; so much representation of the periphery at the centre, that it is not easy to get anything changed. Indeed the periphery is so strongly represented at the centre that it is even inappropriate to speak in those terms. Significant change comes about only after maximum information has been provided and extensive debate has taken place at all levels of the Church's life.

There is a deep suspicion of centralised power and a commitment to the concept of accountability. Presbyterian principles influenced the American constitution with its checks and balances and the division of powers between the President, the Congress and the Supreme Court.

This book is written in response to a request from the publisher. It is gladly, if nervously, written because I believe that the Presbyterian community requires to be understood, and needs at the same time to reflect critically on its position and its future. It is necessary for Presbyterians to take a look at themselves to see whether or not they have been as constructively engaged with the rest of the people of Ireland as they might have been. I will argue in this book that Presbyterians have absorbed the defensive mindset of the wider unionist community to such a degree that they do not always behave in ways which serve their own best interests, or those of other people, never mind the best interests of the Kingdom of God.

It can hardly be denied that Presbyterians are part of a wider Protestant community which frequently, through some of its political representatives, presents a face which appears to many observers to be arrogant, truculent and frequently insensitive. While it may be appropriate to be assertive concerning one's rights, dignity and self-worth, aggressiveness does not serve one's self-interest, never mind that of other people. Nor does it commend the gospel.

As I seek to explain where Presbyterians have come from and why it is that they are as they are, I recognise that there is a danger that explanations become justifications, as if what has happened could not have occurred in any other way. While we often use explanation to describe why we are as we are and in the process attempt to justify ourselves, perhaps implying that we ought not to change, there is, nevertheless, a difference between explanation and justification.

Anyone who does much counselling will recognise that explanation of why one behaves and thinks as one does can easily become a defence of a settled and unmovable conviction that there is only one way of seeing things, and it is not 'hers' or 'his', or 'theirs', as the case may be. While objectivity is claimed and bias may not be intended, it is there nevertheless. If we start justifying everything in terms of what other people either did or failed to do, we lose our own freedom; we cease to be pro-active creative participants in change and we will end up as driftwood washed up on the edges of the activities of other people.

Marianne Elliott wrote on one occasion that both communities in Northern Ireland feel themselves to be victim communities. Both need to be listened to. In Ireland, there is so much pain around that we don't listen too well. We have played zero-sum games in political negotiation, believing that one person's gain is another person's loss. We have done the same when it comes to telling our stories. Stories are weapons in the ideological struggle.

In counselling, I sometimes ask one partner to be quiet while the other speaks. For a person who believes himself or herself to be the wronged partner, to be quiet and to listen is not easy. After some time, I ask the listening person to reflect back as accurately as possible what has been said. The pain is such that this is seldom done with any great degree of accuracy. Only after some time does it become evident that there is often pain on both sides, the victim being also the source of pain. Only through this process does understanding come. An essential part of the process of reconciliation is for stories to be told and to be heard. Hopefully, at the end of the process the person who tells the story will be able to say, 'I have been heard and I have been understood.' When that happens, the individual concerned, or the community concerned, may be able to hear and understand the other part of the overall story which intersects with theirs.

This book has been written not so much to win an argument as to facilitate understanding, so that this Presbyterian community can stand with dignity alongside other communities. In being understood, it may be accommodated and be more accommodating of others for the sake of mutual enrichment. This particular story is not told in order to cancel out someone else's story. All the stories must stand side by side. In Ireland we now have a new opportunity to listen to one another, which may result in creative dialogue rather than in adversarial encounters. As each story is set down, we will create a complex patchwork quilt.

I am sufficiently well acquainted with the deviousness of the human heart to know there are many layers of motivation which goad me to expend the effort into putting these reflections into the public domain. I would like to have the specific particularity of the Presbyterian community recognised, and to have its share of recent trauma and suffering acknowledged. I am also persuaded that this particular community is sufficiently significant that it needs to be taken seriously when anyone speaks about the people of Ireland.

Protestants have been blamed for so much recently, that they find it difficult to take ownership of those matters for which they may reasonably be held responsible. I hope that this book is not without insight into our own deficiencies as a community.

Presbyterians, along with many others in Northern Ireland, have been blasted by twenty-five years of efficient IRA violence. Along with that they have been besieged by rhetoric, and by international interpreters who seem to have been persuaded that there is only one story to be sympathetically heard and that is the Irish Catholic story. That story needs to be told and has often been persuasively told. There are, however, other stories to be heard, of which the Presbyterian story is one. Since these stories intersect, it is my hope that those who do not come from the Presbyterian community will feel that I have attempted to understand their communities as well as my own. Nevertheless, this book is not meant to be a a comprehensive statement about everybody; it is written from a Presbyterian perspective.

The challenge is how to tell this story, which contains elements of achievement, of critical self-examination, and of grievance, without attempting thereby to be the sole occupant of the moral high ground, or failing to acknowledge that, as well as being victims, we have caused other people to be victims.

This book invites the reader to step into my shoes and walk around with a Presbyterian who recognises some of these things and looks into an unpredictable future in which the Presbyterians of Ireland have a constructive and creative part to play.

1

THE MISTRUST OF
CENTRALISED POWER

People in Great Britain know about Cardinal Hume and Archbishop Carey. How many could name the current Moderator of the General Assembly of the Church of Scotland?

People in Ireland know the names of the Catholic Cardinal and the Anglican Archbishop; but few, other than committed Presbyterians and those who need to know, could immediately name any current Moderator of the General Assembly of the Presbyterian Church in Ireland.

The Catholic Church in Ireland has a sustained corporate identity through its current Primate, Cardinal Cahal Daly. The church has a weekly Mass attendance of 3,836,958, of whom 516,500 worship in Northern Ireland.

The Church of Ireland (Anglican) has a similar sustained corporate identity through its current Primate, Archbishop Robin Eames. The Church has an all-Ireland community membership of 371,150 of whom 278,850 live in Northern Ireland.

Many who know of both these leaders and their respective Churches, know little of the existence of the Presbyterian Church in Ireland, which has a community membership of 349,290, of whom an estimated 336,300 live in Northern

Ireland.[1] This makes the Presbyterian Church community larger than the Church of Ireland in Northern Ireland, but few people outside Northern Ireland seem to know of its existence.

It is somewhat strange that this community of people seem to be invisible to so many people. One reason is the absence of an ongoing identifiable leader or spokesperson. The problem lies in the Presbyterian practice of electing a new Moderator of the General Assembly in June each year. No Moderator holds office for more than a year; indeed, by the time a Moderator has established a public identity, the next Moderator has been nominated. (The Presbyterian Church in Ireland shares this practice with most other Reformed Churches.) While this presents considerable problems in public representation and in projecting a consistent corporate image of the Church and of its policies, the custom is unlikely to change. The Moderator is a person without executive power and with limited influence. The Church honours its Moderator because of the office, rather than because of the particular gifts which any particular person may bring to it.

Having chaired the week-long meetings of the General Assembly, the Moderator continues as the Church's principal public representative for one year, during which he may explain what the policy of the Church is on certain issues or may be so bold as to express a personal opinion on any number of other issues. However, the only body which expresses the mind of the Church in a definitive way is the General Assembly itself, a body with as many as twelve hundred elders and ministers which debates and decides matters in the first full week in June each year. It is not usual for them all to be present at the same time, but for controversial matters there will be more than seven hundred present. With the exception of one brief private session, all the business is carried on in public.

On the back of the Moderator's chair are carved the words 'Primus inter pares' (first among equals). Following the year of office the Moderator returns to whatever responsibilities were previously held. He ceases to be 'first among equals' and returns to being nothing more and nothing less than an equal. It has been well said that there is no one more ex than an ex-Moderator. I know of one ex-Moderator who, having handed over to his successor, and having preached at the Assembly communion service on the following morning, left the Assembly, took off his robes and on his return, being unable to find a seat, sat on the nearest windowsill. *Sic transit gloria mundi*, indeed.

While the temporary nature of the office of Moderator may have its drawbacks, one of its strengths is that the Moderator, nominated each year by a majority of the twenty-one presbyteries in Ireland, is identified with the wider Church rather than with any administrative centre. This heightens the credibility of the Moderator when the choice is that of a large number of people, freely given and not the result of some centralised power structure or well-organised caucus.

DEVOLUTION OF POWER TO THE CENTRE

The nominating procedure for Moderators has its roots in Presbyterian commitment to local involvement in decision-making and in an associated suspicion of centralised power, which manifests itself in opposition both to executive bishops and to the giving of responsibility to individuals rather than to boards and committees within the government of the Church. The Presbyterian Church is a complex body with a carefully balanced set of relationships. It is a powerful community of faith which is not dependent upon centralised leadership for its strength.

The Church is one organic unified body comprising the local kirk sessions, through the presbyteries and synods to the General Assembly. A significant amount of responsibility lies at the levels of the kirk sessions and presbyteries.

The local congregation is governed by the kirk session, the

members of which are elected and thereafter ordained for life. The minister of the congregation is the moderator of the kirk session. The Church has permitted women to be ordained as elders since 1926, and in 1973 voted to allow women's ordination as ministers; eighteen presbyteries voted for the motion and three voted against it. The first woman to be ordained was the Reverend Ruth Patterson, in 1976, and there are now twenty-one women ordained as ministers in the Church.

The financial and property affairs of the congregation come under the control of the Church committee, again an elected body, which must present an account of its stewardship, with audited accounts and associated records of contributions, to the annual meeting of the congregation. The committee, unlike the kirk session, must be elected regularly. In order to protect the independence of the minister from local pressure in the exercise of his or her ministry as a preacher and pastor, the minister is accountable to the next level of responsibility, that of the local presbytery, which consists of the ministers and an equal number of elders appointed by the kirk sessions of the congregations within its area of responsibility.

Beyond that are similarly constituted synods and, finally, the General Assembly itself, all the boards and committees of which are balanced with ministers and elders. No one can hold an appointment on any board for more than nine years, which prevents fiefdoms being established. It is a cumbersome and inefficient way of running an organisation the size of the Presbyterian Church in Ireland; even more so with larger Churches like the Church of Scotland or the Presbyterian Church USA.

Such is the regard for the protection of the rights of minorities within the Presbyterian system of Church government, that a majority decision in the General Assembly is not, in itself, enough to effect a change in the constitution of the Church. Such a proposal, having gained a majority in the General Assembly, must then be sent to presbyteries for their approval or disapproval. If a majority of presbyteries approve, it may then be dealt with again at the next Assembly, where it will again require a majority to be passed.

No one can appoint a Presbyterian minister to a congregation. The congregation has the responsibility of making the choice and, provided the procedures are properly followed, the presbytery will then install the minister who is the choice of the people and has received their call. The process is overseen by the presbytery but not controlled by it. This system inculcates in people the conviction that they have the right to be consulted about matters which concern them. Therein lie the seeds of democracy.

Presbyterian ideals have influenced the wider population and they share civic values with many people who are not Presbyterians. They value such ideals as: suspicion of the misuse of centralised power; the importance of accountable democratic institutions; guarantees that minorities should not be overwhelmed by the wishes of democratically elected majorities; fair treatment for such minorities; those holding positions of responsibility should be accountable to the people; people should willingly abide by the law as a civic duty and not through fear of law enforcement; where individuals do not abide by the law they should be amenable to due process of law, otherwise the people will lose confidence in the law enforcement agencies and the judicial system; speech should be straightforward and unambiguous: 'Let your yea be yea and your nay be nay'; there is room for open disagreement and diversity both within the Church and within the wider community.[2]

VIEWS FROM WITHIN AND WITHOUT: IDEALISM AND REALITY

A.T.Q. Stewart is surely right when he writes of the Presbyterian:

> The austere doctrines of Calvinism, the simplicity of his worship, the democratic government of the Church, the memory of the martyred Covenanters, and the Scottish refusal to yield or to

dissemble – all these incline him to that difficult and can-
tankerous disposition which is characteristic of a certain kind
of political radicalism.[3]

Professor J. Ernest Davey was one of the best scholars the
Presbyterian Church has produced. He was also one of the
gentlest of people. At the Tercentenary Celebrations in 1942 he
drew attention to the Presbyterian qualities of:

> courage and endurance, of simplicity and dignity of life and wor-
> ship, of straight dealing, consistency of character, independence
> of mind, and the democratic temper . . . Consistency is perhaps
> the first moral attribute found in the character of God in the
> historical development of ethical theism; and consistency seems
> in the Irish Presbyterian to be a foundation virtue . . .[4]

This internal self-understanding differs from the assessment
of someone from outside the Presbyterian Church. It is worth
quoting Professor J.J. Lee's vigorous and trenchant assessment
of Protestants in general.

> The dedication with which Ulster Protestants laboured to sustain
> a sense of racial superiority in these circumstances itself elo-
> quently expressed the racist cast of their minds . . .
>
> Ulster Protestants fashioned an elaborate set of images to
> sustain their sense of identity . . . In vivid contrast to this self-
> image of sturdy if dour manliness, Irish Catholics conformed in
> Protestant minds to the classic stereotype of the native which set-
> tler races find it psychologically necessary to nurture. They were
> lazy, dirty, improvident, irresolute, feckless, made menacing
> only by their numbers and by their doltish allegiance to a sinister
> and subversive religion.
>
> Ulster Protestants cherished a satisfying sense of individual
> self-reliance which they conveniently confused with individual-
> ism. Genuine individualism made little impact on the herd men-
> tality within fortress Ulster. Nonconformity flourished more as a
> religious label than as an intellectual style.[5]

It would be difficult to find more contrasting assessments of
the same group of people. Without necessarily agreeing with

everything that Professor Lee says, those of us who know Presbyterianism from within know of both an acceptance of and an intolerance of diversity.

What is represented in Professor Davey's assessment of Presbyterian qualities is what is deemed to be best in the tradition. It is a picture of an idealised Presbyterianism, driven by principle. This world of idealism provides a motivating self-definition which imparts a sense of values which themselves can become guidelines for behaviour and provide a touchstone against which deficiencies can be measured. It is important to measure the reality against the idealised world and not to imagine that the idealised world is reality. But while it is true that reality and idealism do not coincide, it would be dishonest to say that idealism is hypocrisy. It does provide a motivating self-definition.

Every Presbyterian hears, at an ordination or installation service, words concerning 'the privilege, right and duty of every man to examine the Scriptures for himself', and 'of the inalienable right of private judgement' and 'the obligation not to set his reason above the Word of God'.[6] By custom, Presbyterians therefore listen to sermons critically, checking what they understand the Word of God to teach with what they are at that moment hearing from the preacher. Presbyterians do not believe in the infallibility of preachers, whatever some of us preachers may believe about ourselves. Some people have difficulty making a distinction, in principle, between what the scriptures teach and what they think they teach, or were told they teach. The understanding of this distinction is important as it engenders within us a humility which is a precondition of a teachable spirit.

This principle of private judgement encourages a culture of suspicion. The trial in 1927 of Professor J. Ernest Davey for heresy made a deep impression on the Church. Five charges were brought against him concerning the grounds of our forgiveness, the perfection of the character of Christ, the inspiration, divine authority and infallibility of scripture, the source of human sinfulness and the doctrine of the Trinity. The Assembly by 707 votes to 82 found in his favour. This happened at the height of the fundamentalist–modernist controversy and excited an enormous amount of interest far beyond Ireland.[7]

Presbyterians continue to be interested in questions of ortho-doxy. Students for the ministry are sometimes encouraged to be overly cautious about what they might be taught in a theological college, even though the General Assembly appoints the pro-fessors. Some students for the ministry seem to go to theological college persuaded that they should not be diverted from what they already believe. There is great emphasis among some people in the Church as to who is 'evangelical and theologically orthodox' and who is not.

Many people know of the Reverend Dr Ian Paisley and think of him as the leader of the Presbyterian Church in Ireland, of which he has never even been a member. He established a church, which he called the Free Presbyterian Church in 1951, which currently has a community membership of 12,720. Dr Paisley, particularly in the earlier days of his ministry, invested a considerable amount of energy attacking the Presbyterian Church in Ireland, happily with a limited amount of success. He still periodically honours the General Assembly by turning up outside to protest.

Dr Paisley has been more successful in dividing political unionism, by the creation of the Democratic Unionist Party, than he has been in dividing the Presbyterian Church. While his party is not as large as the Ulster Unionist Party, his personal vote in European elections remains the highest in Northern Ireland, which means that he must have a significant *political* following among some members of the Presbyterian Church in Ireland.

Dr Paisley's attacks on the other Protestant churches in Ireland have mainly been on the issue of ecumenism. It is likely that the influence which he exercised, mainly on the elders of the Presbyterian Church in Ireland, along with the efficiently organised Campaign for Complete Withdrawal from the World Council of Churches mounted by ministers and elders within the Presbyterian Church itself, combined to establish a majority of 433 to 327 in favour of the Presbyterian Church leaving the World Council of Churches in 1980.[8] I doubt if the vote would have gone as it did had it not been for these factors, along with the World Council's Programme to Combat Racism and the allegations that a link existed between that programme, political liberation movements and terrorism. Given the activities of the IRA in Northern Ireland, the debates took place in a volatile and highly charged atmosphere. That decision was followed in 1989 by a further decision not to join the proposed Council of Churches of Britain and Ireland, the successor body to the British Council of Churches. Thus ended the most divisive and painful experience of my life. It is perhaps worth noting that those ministers who, like myself, had worked with the Church overseas were amongst those most opposed to the severing of these links with other parts of the world Church.

The Presbyterian Church in Ireland was a founding member of the World Council of Churches. The recent withdrawal tendencies do not sit easily in the history of a church with such a long history of missionary work in China, India, Malawi, Kenya, Lebanon, Syria, Israel, Jamaica, Brazil, Malaya, Indonesia, Singapore and Nepal, as well as a number of countries in mainland Europe. It continues as a member of the Irish Council of Churches, the Irish Inter-Church Meeting, the Conference of European Churches, and the World Alliance of Reformed Churches, of which it was also a founding member.

ACCOUNTABILITY

One of the truths which a Presbyterian child learned in Sunday School and at home, was that the chief purpose in life is 'to glorify God and to enjoy Him for ever'.[9] Presbyterians have been dominated by the question of God and what He requires, rather than by the question of the Church and what it might require. It is more serious to have to deal with God than with the Church.

Deep within the Presbyterian psyche there lies a sense of accountability. The people of God are called to exercise their own priesthood in Jesus Christ. This is understood *negatively*, in that, since Jesus is our High Priest, no mediation of any kind is required from any other person in order for an individual to be at peace with God. *Positively*, it means that every person has to deal directly with God, and faith must be expressed in upright and honest living, in worship and in service.

Everything matters.

All of life is to be lived before God and everything ought to be influenced by God, whether it is formal worship, cleaning the house, ploughing a field, keeping a farmyard, riveting steel, applying for grants, from the giving of one's word to completing an undertaking or doing business of any kind. All must be done to the glory of God, since the whole earth belongs to God. The whole of life is integrated under the rubric of living in such a way that God is glorified.

Some people would maintain that Presbyterians are not easy people to do business with; but once the deal is done, that's it! There will be no going back on it. No renegotiation of the terms of the deal is expected when it comes to paying over the money. It might well be asked if everything is in fact included and if everything is brought fearlessly to this touchstone. While this is a significant element in Presbyterian behaviour, it is usually applied to the areas of individual personal morality and personal integrity. It has not always been rigorously applied to wider political issues of social justice.

It is always necessary to ask if the law serves justice. What happens if the law is deficient? How would such an issue be raised? How can legislation facilitate the establishment of a just society? In the nineteenth century, evangelical

Protestants like Wilberforce were prominent in issues of social justice. More recent conservative Protestantism, with its stress on individual salvation and individual accountability, often leaves these wider social issues out of account.

Presbyterians in Ireland, for understandable historical reasons having to do with their often precarious minority position on the island, have been concerned about freedom and political security. They have been less consistently concerned about social justice. While being concerned to express their faith in social witness in the field of education and in the care of alcoholics, senior citizens, the unemployed and young offenders, this is different from the Church being a campaigning body in the political areas of social justice. The Church has responded in a considered way to government proposals, rather than being a body which presses for innovative legislative change.

The issue of when it might be permissible to rebel against a government was addressed in a report to the 1993 General Assembly:

> The reformed tradition has always been wary of revolutionary action, since 'the powers that be are ordained of God'. Calvin even held that 'the worst tyranny is more bearable than no order at all' for it still serves in some sense to hold human society together. Nevertheless, God himself may summon his servants to set the oppressed free, hence Calvinists, historically and today, have often been in the forefront of revolutionary movements. But all such action is fraught with moral ambiguity and danger, and violence can be contemplated only as a last resort. In Reformation teaching the Church as such has a spiritual mandate to resist those in power only where they may try to compel the church organisation or membership to act directly contrary to their faith in Jesus Christ as their paramount Lord or to restrict freedom of worship.[10]

2

THE SCOTTISH CONNECTION

There is nothing unmixed about the population of this island. Every invading force left its mark. Celtic migrations brought people to these shores as early as 1000 BC and in greater numbers from 500 BC to overthrow those who were here before them. The Celts 'left many indelible marks on Ireland and its people . . . the core remains unmistakably Celtic', providing 'a rich inheritance for the whole people of Ireland'.[1] Long before Presbyterians arrived, there were Viking and Anglo-Norman invasions and influences. These contributed to the overall mix and were eventually assimilated: in east Down, for example, many Catholic families are descended from settlers coming from the Norman world. The ancient Gaelic order collapsed in the great convulsions of sixteenth- and seventeenth-century Ireland, which century saw the arrival of new settlers amongst whom were the Presbyterians from Scotland 'of impeccably Celtic ancestry'.[2]

The narrow strip of water which separates north-east Ireland from Scotland has provided an easy means of communication stretching back nine thousand years. The people, the cultures, the language and the religions have intermingled over the centuries. It was across that strip of water that the Presbyterians came to Ireland in the early 1600s. The chances of the eventual assimilation of these immigrants was unlikely, since the Reformation struggles had broken Europe apart, setting nation state against nation state on religious grounds. Our society is scarred by a divided church. Since the seventeenth century, religion has become the key marker in Irish identity. Presbyterians are one element in this mixture.

Before 1603 the eastern seaboard of Ulster had seen numerous relationships develop with Scotland, which was daily within sight and easy reach. In the sixteenth century Ulster was the political centre of the lordship of the MacDonnells which stretched across the sea to Scotland. Presbyterianism came to Ireland with the Scottish settlers in the early 1600s. They came to take advantage of a better life under what they saw to be very advantageous conditions. The Hamilton and Montgomery possessions in north and east Down drew such numbers that a far more substantial bridgehead was established than had been originally planned.

The old Gaelic order having collapsed, the settlers instituted a different social order, clearing forests and building towns like Moneymore 'with the sword in one hand and the axe in the other'. The Gaelic Irish were not totally displaced and many remained as labourers and as tenants to the new landowners: '...the grand plan to separate natives and newcomers had come to nothing...The greatest threat, however, was the smouldering resentment of the native Irish who worked and farmed with the settlers.'[3]

The settlers came to a country depopulated by war, but not devoid of inhabitants.

> Everywhere the native Irish were waiting to be moved or dispossessed, and in the forests lurked the woodkerne, landless men and former soldiers of O'Neill, who threatened the settlements.[4]

/433524

It is a characteristic of communal memory to sift through the stories and remember only those parts which sustain one's own community. It seems that communities find stories of massacre and suffering to be solid material for sustaining community memory and community solidarity, provided that one's own community is the victim community. Selective memory, in turn, feeds contemporary enmity.

The rebellion of 1641 has gone down in the mythology of the Protestant community in a similar, though less sustained and intense way, to that of the story of Cromwell's activities in 1649 in the memory of the Catholic Irish. The settlers were overwhelmed in the rebellion, many being killed while others fled. Jonathan Bardon estimates that perhaps two thirds of the twelve thousand or so who perished before the end of 1641 died of exposure or hunger.[5] While some of the stories of massacre are thought to have been exaggerated, others are well authenticated, like the massacre at Portadown.

Major-General Robert Monro arrived in Carrickfergus in April 1642 and went southwards with his Scottish army to quell the rebellion. No quarter was given on either side. One cannot read the account of the suppression of that rebellion without being shocked by the methods which were employed:

> ... he simply slaughtered his captives, first at Kilwarlin Wood, then at Loughbrickland and finally at Newry, where, after shooting and hanging sixty men, he did stop his soldiers throwing women in the river and using them as targets, though only after several had been killed. The rebels hid in the woods, so in marching north again, he seized their cattle and slaughtered any Irish men, women and children that he found.[6]

In 1642 the first presbytery was formed at Carrickfergus by the chaplains and elders of Monro's Scottish army. The presbytery then exercised oversight of the already existing Presbyterian congregations, which were keen to be associated with it. The supply of ministers was very limited and had to be supplemented by a 'short term' scheme of secondment from Scotland.

RD

The Scots who came to Ulster under the Plantation policy did not come on a religious crusade to take possession of the land. It was not led by a Moses or an Aaron 'in the name of the Lord'. The ministers of the Church were not the designated leaders of the settlers. Some ministers, like Robert Blair, came because they objected to the imposition by the King of principles inconsistent with Reformed practice upon the Church in Scotland.

The Presbyterian Church aimed her mission in Ireland primarily at making disciples of the Ulster Scots in their settlements. Where they went, the Church followed. When they retreated or moved, the churches closed. Alistair Kennedy traced this movement:

> After the wars of Elizabeth's reign many parts of Ulster . . . were devastated and almost unpopulated. Scotland had a surplus of population looking for a living and younger sons of the gentry looking for lands . . . Scottish settlers were drifting across to Antrim and Down even before the great Plantation scheme . . .

After 1642 the Presbyterian Church began to expand as presbyteries were established and renewed immigration took place. It changed from a frontier mission to a Church with a solid foundation. Many new congregations were established between 1655 and 1659, by which time there were perhaps 217,000 Presbyterians in Ulster. The five presbyteries of Down, Antrim, Route (North Antrim), Laggan (East Donegal) and Tyrone had by then been formed. As settlers moved inland, so the Church followed the people. The settlers moved first. It was not until after the Williamite war that Presbyterian churches were formed in Monaghan and Cavan, following the heavy loss of lands by Catholic landowners.

The intention was to have a congregation available in every part of Ulster. By the middle of the last century the Presbyterian population had grown to its historic maximum of 642,000. It was still largely rural, supported not merely by agriculture but more significantly by the domestic linen industry; spinning and hand-loom weaving.[7]

It has always been the custom for the Presbyterian Church to follow the people. First it was to the country, then to the urban centres and then to the suburbs of those cities. In this sense the Presbyterian Church is a predominantly ethnic church, mainly of the Scots-Irish. Given the antipathy between the settlers and the native Irish and between the Presbyterian, Anglican and Catholic Churches, and given the identification between religion and ethnicity, it is unlikely that it could have been substantially otherwise.

There were exceptions, like Jeremiah O'Quin, a native Irishman who was ordained as a Presbyterian minister in Billy near Bushmills in 1646, and it is true to say that the Church did try to cross some of the frontiers. A survey indicated that in 1717 eleven ministers and three licentiates were able to preach in Irish. (Some ministers preached in Scots Gaelic, then very little different from Ulster Irish.)

Those who came were often poor; like most migrants, they were people looking for some betterment. Anglican settlers came from the north of England. The strength of Protestant Churches still indicates where the various denominational groups settled. For example today, in 1995, there are nine Presbyterian ministers working in County Monaghan but only three in County Fermanagh.

Rory Fitzpatrick in his book *God's Frontiersmen* paints a picture of hard-working tenant farmers jostling with penniless adventurers, who were probably the younger sons of small landowners, travelling from Scotland with Calvinistic preachers and horse-thieves.[8] Many were soon to learn to fear God. James Seaton Reid wrote of how the zealous labours of the ministers were visibly blessed. The fame of what became known as the Six Mile Water Revival of 1625 spread even to America:

A remarkable improvement in the habits and demeanour of the people was speedily effected. The thoughtless were roused to serious inquiry on the subject of religion, and the careless were alarmed, and, at the same time, urged to self-examination. The profane were, in great measure, silenced, and the immoral reclaimed, while the obstinate opposers of the Gospel were converted into its willing and decided supporters.[9]

These early settlers were supplemented later, in the 1690s, by thousands more people from Scotland, this time fleeing from poor harvests in Scotland, during which it is estimated a quarter of the population may have died.[10]

> Edward Synge, Bishop of Tuam, estimated that fifty thousand Scots families came to Ulster between 1689 and 1715; this figure is probably too high but the Presbyterians were able to record a doubling of their congregations between 1660 and 1715. Bishop McMahon wrote in 1714: 'Although all Ireland is suffering, this province is worse off than the others, because of the fact that from the neighbouring country of Scotland, Calvinists are coming over here daily in large groups of families, occupying the towns and villages, seizing the farms in the richer parts of the country and expelling the natives.'[11]

In the Plantation process, issues of justice and the rights of the previous inhabitants do not seem to have figured. It was an opportunity to be taken and was not seen to be different from plantation opportunities in other parts of the world.

It is important, when Irish Presbyterians consider their history, that they reflect upon the effect which their coming to this country had upon the people who were here before they arrived. Televised reports of the contemporary dispossession of one group of people of their land and their means of livelihood by another group ought to make it easier for us to read history with the emotions engaged as well as the mind. It might lead to a sympathetic understanding of what happened to those who were on the losing side.

THE PRESBYTERIAN QUESTION IN IRELAND

The religious persuasion of the Scottish settlers and their

adherence to deeply held Presbyterian principles caused problems for the authorities. From early on it became clear that there were three religious communities in Ireland, the Catholics, the Anglicans and the Dissenters, which was the name by which Presbyterians were often known.

The restoration of the monarchy in 1660–61, after Cromwell, was followed by the restoration of established episcopal churches. This meant that Presbyterian and other ministers who had been parish ministers in the Cromwellian period lost their livings. Sixty-one Presbyterian ministers were evicted and presbyteries were only able to meet clandestinely. However, the Crown and English interest in Ireland could not afford to alienate the substantial Scots and Presbyterian population and so a connived toleration was reached with a royal grant for Presbyterian ministers, the *regium donum*, paid from 1672 onwards.

In 1689, when the army of King James was proceeding northwards, ravaging the country, many of the Presbyterians fled to Derry, Enniskillen or Scotland. There followed the siege of Derry and the Battle of the Boyne, with significance for all of Europe, and defeat for some in Ireland and victory for others.

Following the Williamite Settlement after the 1690 war, the Presbyterians' position remained anomalous. They had no legal security but enjoyed a sort of unofficial recognition by King William III in an enhanced *regium donum*.

In 1704 under the terms of the Sacramental Test Act, Presbyterians were debarred from taking office under the Crown unless they took communion in the Anglican Church at least once a year. The validity of Presbyterian marriages was not fully and legally recognised until 1845. For the greater part of the eighteenth century Presbyterians were second-class citizens in Ulster. All these experiences made them distrustful of political authority and were instrumental in the eventual alliance of some Presbyterians with Catholics in the United Irishmen.

The treatment of Presbyterians at the hands of the Anglican

Ascendancy is fading in contemporary Presbyterian memory, although people in the country still talk about their predecessors having to pay tithes to the Established Church. It was still very much alive in the folk memory and oratory of the Reverend Professor R.L. Marshall when he preached in 1942 at the three hundredth anniversary of the establishment of the first presbytery. In his words, the record of the Presbyterian Church in Ireland was one of:

> growth and persecution, of long-sustained efforts on the part of the State and of the Protestant Established Church to exterminate it; of boycott and social ostracism; of legal exclusion from offices of State, from Corporations, from the Bench, and from all positions under the Crown.
>
> Presbyterians could starve and die in the Siege of Derry and such a service was permitted and even grudgingly acknowledged; but no Presbyterian was fit to be that city's civic servant. All over the land they were haled before the Bishops' Courts for taking part in Presbyterian worship or Communion; their preachers were gaoled and fined; some of their humble meeting-houses, built not by the State but by their own sacrifice, were levelled or boarded up; their children were branded as illegitimates, and their wives with an evil name . . .
>
> In the outer hall of the church in which I worship [First Derry], a simple tablet on the wall records the names of twenty-four Presbyterians, ejected from the City's Corporation after the Siege of Derry because they refused to perjure their consciences by obedience to the iniquitous Test Act of 1704. It is only one of many that might have been erected. But no one can pass that bare, uncomplaining record without the flame of courage and faith in the future flaring higher.[12]

COMPETITION, SCHISM AND UNION

The present General Assembly of the Presbyterian Church in Ireland represents the union in 1840 of two strands of Presbyterianism and contains in its history a painful schism within the old Synod of Ulster. It is important to appreciate that Presbyterianism is like a piece of wood with a short grain: it is inclined to split under the pressure of perceived principle.

The transmigration of large numbers of Scottish Presbyterians to Ulster brought with it some attitudes and convictions forged in Scotland. In Scotland a Secession had occurred from the Church of Scotland, with its roots in the protest of 1773 against the right of a patron to determine the choice of a minister, and in support of the interests of spiritual life and freedom. The dispute led to the creation of a separate synod, the people involved being known as the Seceders. Some Seceders moved to Ireland and began to organise congregations which were formed into the Secession Synod. The first Secession congregation was established at Lylehill in Co. Antrim in 1746.

Alistair Kennedy described the Seceders' activity as introducing a 'free market' into Presbyterianism. When a long vacancy occurred in a congregation, or there was disagreement over which minister should be called to fill a vacancy (often in those days such disagreements had to do with issues of orthodoxy), the opportunities for disputes within a congregation 'gave occasion for a disgruntled group to invite Seceding preachers into the area . . . The Seceders were, like some modern successors, generally willing to fish in troubled waters.'[13] However, they also went to areas where there was no existing Presbyterian congregation and helped to fill in the gaps in the geographical spread of Presbyterianism. There were eventually more than one hundred Secession congregations, practically all of them in Ulster. The Secession Synod eventually united with the Synod of Ulster in 1840, but only after a schism had taken place within that synod over the issue of subscription to the Westminster Confession of Faith, which was also a dispute about orthodoxy and freedom.

This issue convulsed Irish Presbyterianism for decades; split congregations before splitting the synod; produced two towering figures within Presbyterianism in the persons of Henry

Montgomery and Henry Cooke;[14] and eventually produced the Nonsubscribing Presbyterian Church.

Undoubtedly, as Professor J. Ernest Davey observed: 'By the schism Presbyterianism lost many persons of culture, of wealth, of public spirit and philanthropic zeal . . .',[15] but it is also true that the victory of the orthodox party, led by Henry Cooke, which was in favour of ministers being required to subscribe to the Westminster Confession of Faith, paved the way for the eventual union of the Secession Synod with the Synod of Ulster to form the General Assembly of the Presbyterian Church in Ireland in 1840. This union would probably not have taken place had the subscription issue not been resolved in favour of the orthodox party.[16]

This tendency to split over perceived principle is significant in understanding Presbyterians. At one time in the early 1800s there were no fewer than six bodies all claiming to represent the true genius of Presbyterianism: the General Synod of Ulster, the Presbytery of Antrim, the Seceder Burghers, the Seceder anti-Burghers, James Bryce's Associate Presbytery and the Reformed Presbyterians. A similar tendency to split over principle was evident in Scotland in what was known as 'the Disruption' of 1843. The dispute had to do with the right of a congregation to call its own minister. It split the Church in Scotland in two. One has to be aware of the risks and sacrifices involved for those who took this course of action. They had to leave the buildings in which they worshipped and the manses in which they lived, without compensation being available. They then erected churches, manses, schools and colleges throughout Scotland. Similar divisions took place in Reformed churches in Holland, the Swiss Cantons and in France. Lutheranism and Anglicanism have known nothing like this.[17]

The Presbyterian people who live in Ireland have connections with the Presbyterianism of Scotland and the rest of the world. There is a well-established tendency to divide rather than to accommodate conflicting diversity when a perceived betrayal of principle is involved. They are a difficult people to deal with. In ecumenical relations in Ireland some people from other denominations find Presbyterian representatives careful to the point of exasperation. They tend not to move until they are convinced that to move to some new position is warranted by the evidence and authorised by the General Assembly.

Anyone who thinks that these people from this tradition are going to be domesticated and turned into easy-going people who will agree to nearly anything, does not appreciate that the traditions which inform their lives have been with them for some hundreds of years. They will not be worn down into a uniformity which destroys their particularity. If they are recognised for what they are and are given space to be true to themselves, they may well co-operate with others; but they will not do it if their particularity is discounted.

The churches on the Protestant side of the community in Ireland are deeply fractured. There are tensions within denominations as well as between them. The history of Protestantism shows that theological issues take priority over unity issues: hence the distrust of ecumenism among some members of the Presbyterian Church in Ireland. Unity is conditional on theological agreement. Churches split or remain separated when people are unable to agree theologically.

However, while formal Church unity is clearly conditional on substantial theological agreement, that does not rule out the possibility of co-operation without compromising the integrity of the particularity of different Churches. While the position of the Presbyterian Church in Ireland on ecumenism is cautious, it has within its membership many individuals who are supportive, on principle, of ecumenism; it also has many people who are opposed to it, on principle. It is, however, agreed by everyone that there can never be formal union until there is adequate theological agreement, and that is not in sight.

For some people however, not only is any form of co-operation out of the question, even association is frowned upon.

As one minister told me concerning his reluctance to be present at a public function which was to be attended by local priests, 'Some of my elders would not like to see my photograph in the local paper along with priests.' While it might be said by way of explanation that his pastoral relationships with the elders at that time took priority over the other matter, it demonstrates that the independence of the minister may be constrained by the need to remain pastorally sensitive to the convictions or indeed the prejudices of some elders.

3

PRESBYTERIANS AND THEIR
CATHOLIC NEIGHBOURS

DISPARITIES IN SIZE

It probably surprises Catholics to know that Protestants are preoccupied about them in a way that is not reciprocated. They might ask why we should be concerned about them at all. The simple answer to that is that Catholics constitute such a massive majority in Ireland.

Looked at from the viewpoint of a neighbour, the Catholic Church in Ireland appears to be threateningly powerful: the vast numbers; the centralised power and the international connections; the churches, schools, hospitals, seminaries, colleges, convents and retreat houses; and an estimated 84.5 per cent attendance at Mass, constituting over 3,800,000 worshippers every weekend. The Catholic community represents power and this not only in numerical strength. It is gifted academically, with international scholarship of a high calibre. It continues to produce people of singular dedication who serve in places far from home, requiring deep commitment. I regularly meet priests now serving in Ireland who for years have been on the missions, often in remote and demanding situations.

The Church's 'option for the poor' means that some priests and religious orders struggle alongside and on behalf of the poor in the inner cities of the world. The present Pope is conservative, but as well as working to undermine communism, he has raised serious questions about capitalist consumerism. The Catholic Church has managed to stay in touch more successfully than has the Presbyterian Church in Ireland with the more deprived sections of society in Belfast, although I suspect that, with the secular urbanisation of cities, this aspect of their work will become more difficult.

The estimated 84.5 per cent attendances at Mass are remarkably high. In contrast to that, the active Church membership of those claiming connection with the Irish Presbyterian community of 349,000 is estimated at 58 per cent.[1] Perhaps as few as 60 per cent of the 'active' Presbyterian membership would attend worship every week. I am not complaining about the high percentage of Catholics who go to Mass; I wish it were matched by the Presbyterians. What interests me here is the difference in numbers.

My Catholic friends acknowledge the differential in size, but wonder why it should be threatening. I remember one Methodist minister remarking that Presbyterians, who had a number of strong congregations in the town where he worked, carried on as if the Methodists did not exist. The Methodists found this quite intimidating. The powerful tend not to ask themselves how they appear to those who are less strong.

Peter Hebblethwaite in *The Year of Three Popes* tells of the discussions which he had during Vatican II with Albino Luciani who was to become Pope John Paul I.

> His greatest difficulty with the Council, he freely admitted, was caused by its declaration *On Religious Freedom*. He had been taught by Cardinal Ottaviani in the Belluno seminary that 'error had no rights' and that, consequently, the toleration of Protestants was impossible where Catholics were in a majority. This illiberal doctrine – traceable to Pio Nono and his *Syllabus of Errors* – evidently cut at the root of ecumenism. It was challenged at the

Council . . . Luciani pondered the matter and changed his mind. He said later: 'I studied the question in depth and reached the conclusion that we had been wholly wrong.'

What he came to understand in the discussions was that if there was to be religious liberty for Catholics then they, in turn, had to grant the same liberty to non-Catholics. This meant that people who were held to be in error still had rights which had to be recognised. In the light of such pre-Vatican II convictions it is easier to understand the historic anxieties of Ireland's Protestant minorities.[2]

Within Ireland, the relationships between the Catholic and Presbyterian Churches are improving in many places. The number of interchurch conferences and services which are organised gives some indication of the thawing of these relationships. These meetings, and the informal contacts which flow from them, give us an opportunity to learn about each other and to speak frankly to one another.

The openness of the Catholic community to Protestants often takes Protestants by surprise. The way Presbyterian Irish Mission workers are received in many Catholic schools indicates more interest in the scriptures than is often evidenced in the controlled sector of Education in Northern Ireland which has quite close connections with the Protestant Churches. I remember the warmth of the invitation extended to me by Fr Christopher McCarthy to preach in Clonard Church and to say 'whatever I thought the Holy Spirit wanted me to say'.

What surprised me at a 1994 *Studies* conference on the future of the Catholic Church in Ireland was the sense of deepening crisis within it.[3] This has been occasioned by a number of factors, including the rapid social changes taking place in the Republic of Ireland; the fall-off in attendance at Mass by younger educated people and the urban poor; the reduction in the numbers of men and women offering for the priesthood and the religious life; the publicised scandals involving a few priests;

and the vocal demands of well-informed women to be involved at the centre of the Church's life.

From the outside, the Catholic Church looks not only large, but also monolithic and unified. On closer acquaintance, one finds that there is diversity of many kinds within the Church. I know that there is debate behind the walls about celibacy; about the present Pope, the previous ones and the next one; about the need for consultation and the involvement of the laity in decision making. The trouble is that the internal debate has not been aired sufficiently widely in the press and on radio and television for the rest of us to know what is going on. A book like Joseph Dunn's *No Lions in the Hierarchy* helps to open up the Catholic Church for those of us who do not belong to it.[4]

While the Catholic Church remains structurally hierarchical, the internal shift of emphasis from 'institution' to 'community of believers', with increasing stress on themes like the unconditional love of God and on fellowship, forgiveness and hope place the Catholic Church much nearer to Protestantism than used to be the case.

However, the vexed question of mixed or interchurch marriages remains an emotive issue. Speaking in 1983 at an International Consultation on Interchurch Marriages organised by the Irish School of Ecumenics in Dublin, Garret FitzGerald said that 'as a result of mixed marriage, an erosion of the Protestant population by about 25 per cent per generation had occurred. The fact is that more than any other single factor, the observed decline in the Protestant population in the Republic has confirmed Northern Protestants in their prejudices and fears. Northern Protestants find distasteful a society in which the influence of the Roman Catholic Church in a given population situation has the observed effect of decimating the Protestant population there.'

Garret FitzGerald refers in his autobiography to the halving of the Protestant population in the Republic of Ireland due to this factor and to his unsuccessful attempts to get the Papal

Secretary of State, Archbishop Casaroli, to see the importance of doing something about it.[5] The interests and priorities of Rome seem to be paramount, regardless of the impact of the policies on those who do not belong. How is it that the Presbyterian religious heritage of so many people like John Hume and Garret FitzGerald has been dissolved in the potent mix of Irish Catholic Nationalism? It was not that such weakening of the already fragile non-Catholic sector of southern society was the intention; it was an unintended consequence of the Catholic Church being true to its powerful self.

Recent more sensitive interpretation of the mixed marriage regulations has mitigated some of the more difficult problems. The situation varies from place to place and from diocese to diocese. Some priests want no more than an undertaking that the children will be raised as Christians. The current practice of an interchurch marriage taking place in the bride's church, unless both partners wish it to be otherwise, is very welcome. Even though only the Catholic partner is required to make promises about the upbringing of children, and even though those promises cannot unilaterally determine the final decision, it would be very helpful if the Church would cease entirely the practice of requiring promises and leave the matter to the couple concerned.

INTERCHURCH RELATIONS

I welcome serious theological dialogue between world confessional Church bodies, searching out areas of agreement and disagreement, thereby diminishing areas of confusion. The Report of the Reformed/Roman Catholic International Dialogue 1984–1990 stated:

> ... we have sought further to clarify the common ground between our communions as well as to identify our remaining differences ... We are moving closer to being able to write our histories together.

Dialogue and increased understanding do not mean that 'all problems between Reformed and Roman Catholic Churches have been resolved; it is to say that a search for solutions is under way, and being undertaken by both sides'.[6]

The Presbyterian Church in Ireland's statement about agreements and disagreements with Catholics stated:

> While Presbyterians rejoice in the better relations which are now experienced between Roman Catholics and Protestants in general, e.g. participation together in prayer and bible study, they do not see much evidence of the radical changes that would be necessary to make any significant reconciliation between our two Churches possible, but we must always remember that with God, all things are possible.[7]

No good comes from either minimising the degree of greater understanding and more frequent contact or, on the other hand, minimising the degree of theological divergence which still exists. To fail in the first, is to be less than truthful. To fail in the second is to invite the accusation that the whole ecumenical exercise is based on deception. The challenge lies in recognising what we have in common, affirming and celebrating its significance and at the same time recognising that there is diversity which cannot and must not and should not be willed away, suppressed or denied. I would welcome an official Irish dialogue between the Presbyterian Church and the Catholic Church so that we could produce a common document on the matters about which we agree and disagree. It would prevent misrepresentation.

A very helpful joint document resulted from 'The Evangelical–Roman Catholic Dialogue on Mission'.[8] Those of us who were privileged to participate in a conference in Corrymeela based on this document found that Fr Kevin MacDonald, from the Vatican Secretariat for Christian Unity, who was a last minute substitute for Msgr Basil Meeking, was very sensitive to and well-informed about, not only Reformed theology in general, but about the evangelical emphases within it.

SECTARIANISM

In these discussions, and indeed in books like this one, one runs the risk of offending people and misrepresenting them. While that is not done intentionally, it is only as these matters are put on the table and discussed that misunderstandings can be removed.

I found Fionnuala O Connor's *In Search of a State: Catholics in Northern Ireland* both fascinating and depressing. My general impression is that the Catholic community in Northern Ireland is at present possessed of a greater sense of self-confidence and hope than the Protestant community. However, few contributors had anything of a very positive nature to say either about the Church to which I belong or about the wider Protestant community of which I am a part. My conclusion was that if this is where we are at as a community, we are still in serious trouble. Clearly the lines of rupture run very deep.[9]

The stories of three people give me cause to pause and reflect.

Professor Mary McAleese, a Belfast Catholic, wrote in the *Belfast Telegraph* on 14 November 1994:

> Even though I was brought up here and wanted to belong, I had a sense of not being fully welcomed. I was very conscious that we were regarded as subversive, because of the community from which we came.
>
> I will probably go to my grave not knowing how an entire community could be written off and their history damaged and distorted by that label.

Another Catholic, Alex Atwood, wrote in the *Belfast Telegraph* on the following day:

> Belfast gives me a sense of home and calls on those who consider the city 'home' to forge a common struggle on our common problems.

I remember being spat on and abused on bus journeys home from school by pupils from a different school; of masked UDA men facing our home and fear being tangible.

From childhood to adulthood, countless experiences told me that while I lived here, somehow I was a threat to be confronted.

A Catholic friend recounted the following story. He was raised in Belfast, but moved on promotion with his family to Dublin. He went to Lansdowne Road to see the Republic of Ireland play Northern Ireland at soccer. Coming from Belfast, it had been his custom to support Northern Ireland. With his experience of Dublin, he was unsure, before the match, which side to support. About half-an-hour into the match, the matter had resolved itself in favour of the Republic. Reflecting afterwards on what had happened, he came to the conclusion that, faced with that choice, he had found it impossible to support a team coming from a part of Ireland in which he had never been made to feel fully at home or accepted.

Presbyterians cannot be happy with a situation where people, who have every right to feel at home in this part of the country, tell us that they do not do so.

I don't need to be told about Presbyterian young people who have been spat at and stoned and chased by pupils from Catholic schools. I know all about that. While we have to try to control our children, there has to be an aim, beyond that of control and restraint, of positive accommodation and respect, so that it does not occur to children to be involved in this kind of behaviour. Integrated education and Education for Mutual Understanding programmes all help along that road.

Patrick Speight asked me one morning on *Sunday Sequence* on BBC Radio Ulster if the Protestant community would feel a sense of shame after the Greysteel killings by loyalists which had happened the previous evening, 30 October 1993. My reply was something to the effect that I didn't think most people in the Protestant community would identify themselves with those who carried out that atrocity and would therefore not feel shame. I have always believed that there was a very limited amount of support in the Protestant community for loyalist paramilitaries.

Afterwards, I wondered if I and my community were disowning too easily any relationship with, or responsibility for, the people who were involved. I know none of them nor do I know anything about any Church connections they may have. It is, however, likely that those young men may have gone to the Sunday Schools of some Protestant Church or attended a school with Protestant Church connections. There are subtle cobwebs of prejudice which all of us have both spun and been caught up in.

The Irish Inter-church Meeting's discussion document on sectarianism suggested that sectarianism is like a pyramid. At the TOP are the activities of the paramilitary 'mad dogs' whose activities are condemned by nearly everyone at lower levels.

This top paramilitary level rests upon the MIDDLE level of people who use platform, pulpit or the pages of the press to express bigoted or inflammatory sentiments. They condemn violence, but stir up hatred.

In turn, this middle level could not survive without the tacit support on the GROUND level of many 'ordinary decent people' who have some sympathy for their views. By private opinion, vote or religious view they encourage the layer above them. Such people would be horrified to be told that they are connected with the violent layer at the top. Yet it is not hard to see how each layer of the pyramid depends upon the one below it.[10]

This stimulating discussion document challenges us to be careful about how we think, speak and act, lest we be the inadvertent supporters of the layer above the one where we normally locate ourselves and, therefore, are numbered among those who help to create the conditions required for violence to be fostered or tolerated. Sectarianism is a kind of virus which infects all of us.

If we have a responsibility to be concerned about the wellbeing of people other than ourselves, then we have to do everything we can to create a society which accommodates religious and cultural diversity, so that people feel at home in a place in which they have every right to feel at home. No doubt explanations can be offered, which are not without some justification, as to how the nationalist community in Northern Ireland contributed to the process which brought about the alienation which they have experienced, and I will attempt that explanation shortly.

However, Presbyterians must accept their fair share of responsibility for allowing that amount of alienation to occur. In community relations terms such division has been disastrous; it has had serious political consequences which are related to the violence, and, judged against the gospel criteria of the obligation to love our neighbours and our enemies, it means we have failed to a serious degree.

It is clearly unsatisfactory that we have permitted a society to be created where so many people say they have been made to feel that they do not belong. I do not believe that either one of our two communities is blameless. In whatever proportions the blame might be apportioned, the present situation needs to be rectified and we have a part to play in it.

What concerns me now is whether Presbyterians are prepared to be a part of a process which may change this society for the better, or to be a part of a process which continues to prevent people feeling at home. To do nothing is to acquiesce in the continuance of the status quo: can any Christian really want this?

The 'Peace Vocation' of the Presbyterian Church, circulated to Church members in 1994, made it clear where the Church stands on this issue:

WE, MEMBERS OF THE PRESBYTERIAN CHURCH IN IRELAND,
called by God,
in the grace of Jesus Christ,
and the power of the Holy Spirit,

to live in faith, hope and love,
as children of our heavenly Father,
and witnesses to God's Kingdom,
publicly acknowledge our vocation to peace,
which is both the gift and mission placed on us by God.

WE BELIEVE that the same evangelical faith in Jesus Christ,
which emboldens us to pray to God as our heavenly
    Father,
challenges us to develop radically new attitudes and
    relationships
with our neighbours in Ireland.

WE AFFIRM that to be Christian peacemakers in our own
    situation:
We must grasp more clearly the distinctive teaching of
    our Lord
which challenges the general practice of our world,
and breaks the vicious cycle of matching injury with injury,
hate with hate, ignorance with ignorance.
We must therefore be prepared to meet and talk together:
with those in our own church with whom we have
    disagreements;
with those from churches whose practices and beliefs differ
    from our own;
with those from whom we are politically divided.

WE AFFIRM that to be Christian peacemakers in our own
    situation:
we must recognise the responsibility given by God to
    government,
and to those who serve the cause of law and order,
so as to encourage well doing, correct evil-doers, and protect
    the innocent.
We must therefore reject violence;
seek ways to advance justice and promote the welfare of
    the needy;
affirm that in democratic societies all citizens are called
to share in these responsibilities;

and encourage all efforts to establish new structures of consent
and participation.

WE AFFIRM that to be Christian peacemakers in our own situation:
We must be initiators of programmes of action
which will contribute to peace in our community.
We must therefore provide resources and encouragement to
enable congregations to move forward at the local level in
the field of inter-community relations.

WE UNDERSTAND peacemaking to be an affirmation
and accommodation of diversity,
and that our particular history in this land of divided
    communities and recurring violence,
of mutual suspicion, fear and injury,
makes it imperative that we reassert the Church's own proper
    calling
to seek peace, and the things that make for peace
in our day.

4

CHANGING RELATIONSHIPS
OVER CENTURIES

TEMPORARY ALLIANCES

Nationalists like Mary McAleese and Alex Atwood find difficulty in understanding why the whole of the nationalist community is looked upon with suspicion. The reasons lie deeply imbedded within the historical experience of insecurity.

As previously discussed, in 1704, under the terms of the Sacramental Test Act, Presbyterians were debarred from taking office under the Crown, or from holding commissions in the army or the militia, unless they took communion in the Anglican Church at least once per year. For the greater part of the eighteenth century Presbyterians were second-class citizens in Ulster, Catholics being third-class. All these experiences made them distrustful of political authority.

Towards the end of the eighteenth century there occurred that alliance of some Presbyterians and some Catholics which resulted in the formation of the United Irishmen. Presbyterians in Dublin and in Belfast had a part to play in that creative movement in Irish history.

Presbyterians from Belfast like Dr William Drennan, the son of the minister of the First Presbyterian Church in Rosemary Street, who was the real founder of the United Irishmen, and including Henry Joy McCracken and Samuel Neilson, whose families were members of the congregation of which I am now the minister, were active in the movement which sought to bring Dissenters, Anglicans and Catholics together under the common name of Irishmen. Henry Joy McCracken was attended, prior to his execution, by his minister, the Reverend Sinclair Kelburn.[1] Mr Kelburn was himself imprisoned in Kilmainham on suspicion of being implicated in the rebellion, though he was later released, partly due to the representations made by 162 members of the congregation testifying that he was never connected with any political society whatsoever. He never recovered his health after the experience.[2]

This movement was to some degree rooted in the common Dissenting/Catholic experience of being denied dignity and a place in the decision-making processes of their own society, an important factor in the formation of the alliance. Another element was the influence of ideas which had come to the fore in the American War of Independence and later in the French Revolution with its cry of 'liberty, equality and fraternity'.

The Presbyterian connection with America was strong. During the eighteenth century as many as 250,000 Presbyterians may have emigrated to America. They constituted that first significant wave of emigration from Ireland which predated by a century the later Catholic emigrations at the time of the Famine.[3] Most Presbyterian families in Ireland at that time had relations in America. The number of Presidents descended from the Scots-Irish is disputed, but one estimate is that at least ten American Presidents are of direct Scots-Irish descent.[4]

As well as family connections with North America there were strong trading links, along with the interchange of ideas. Over three hundred Irish Presbyterian ministers, ordained in the eighteenth century, had been trained in Scotland in the philosophy and social policy of Francis Hutcheson, the son of the Reverend John Hutcheson, minister of Downpatrick and later of Armagh. Francis Hutcheson taught Francis Alison who later became Vice-Provost of the University of Philadelphia and he in turn taught 50 per cent of those who signed the American Declaration of Independence. The ideas of the 'Rights of Man and the Sovereign People' were later believed by the United Irishmen to be strong enough concepts to overcome the religious divide in Ireland. These rights were for everyone. These concepts gave people a universe of concern which was wider than a universe circumscribed by the limits of a denomination.

When the American revolution broke, the sympathy of many northern Presbyterians lay with the colonists:

> Denied access to Trinity College Dublin, Presbyterians took degrees in medicine and divinity at Edinburgh and Glasgow, then perhaps the most open-minded universities in Europe. The Enlightenment had taken deep root in Belfast . . .[5]

Radical Presbyterianism expressed itself in social action and in demands for reform and the representation of all the people. The intention of the movement was to achieve its aims by constitutional means but the suppression of the movement became so intense and the resistance to reform so obdurate that those favouring violent rebellion won the argument, resulting in the United Irishmen rebellion of 1798. It was suppressed with the utmost cruelty.[6]

This unusual and brief alliance of people from different backgrounds illustrates the fact that an understanding of and commitment to justice is often found among those people whose perceptions of justice are directly related to their experiences of its absence.

It is well expressed by Mark Hannan:

> For some of us, justice is a word we use . . . But for others justice is an experience – that must be endured. Or rather, the absence of justice. For it does not need a concept, a word carefully defined and correctly spelt, to remind us that justice is not ours. It is something that we have not got but know that we want;

something we never had, but know we have been denied;
something whose presence is longed for, and whose absence is
daily felt. When we are written off, abused or put down . . . then
we know that justice is more than a word. And we know even
more clearly that injustice is more than a negation, it is pain, it
is oppression, it is a destroyer of dignity.[7]

God's truth is not discovered in the solitude of the study
alone. It is only when the sharp and incisive Word of God is permitted to cut through the flesh to the bone of contemporary
reality that we know what the Word of God and its associated
truth might be. It is not good enough for a preacher to engage
in exposition of scripture which is unrelated to what is going on
outside the study and the church building. All that may be happening in such preaching is that the people are being well
schooled in their understanding of what happened in some
other place at another time, with studious avoidance of any application of its relevance to contemporary issues. It is to the
credit of some evangelicals in present-day Ireland that they are
attempting to relate the faith to contemporary society. The relevant reflective studies which they have produced under the
name of ECONI (Evangelical Contribution on Northern Ireland)
are very helpful in applying the scriptures to our contemporary
difficulties.

It would be inaccurate to imply that the whole Presbyterian
community supported the United Irishmen. A.T.Q. Stewart
maintains that there was little support outside Dublin, Belfast,
south Antrim and north Down. It had no support in the areas
which had been most affected by the 1641 rebellion,[8] and
strongest support where Catholics were so few in number that
they posed no threat.

The attacks on Protestants during the 1798 rebellion had an
effect on northern Presbyterian opinion, reviving the old fears
and, like all such violence since, eventually led to alliances
between Anglicans and Presbyterians against a perceived and
explicit common threat.

However, the radical strain in Presbyterianism survived the after-effects of the 1798 rebellion. In 1813 the Synod of Ulster gave 'official if qualified support to the Catholic cause'. But later attempts were made, unsuccessfully, to rally the Presbyterians against the cause of Catholic Emancipation. The year 1829 saw the failure of an attempt to get the required minimum of at least two presbyteries to call upon the moderator of synod to convene a special meeting of the synod which might 'petition the King and legislature against further concessions of political power to Roman Catholics'. The presbytery of Ballymena was the only one to vote in favour.[9]

Industrialisation and the collapse of Ulster's rural economy from 1820 to the end of the 1840s brought rural Protestants from mid and western Ulster, where they had lived as Protestant minorities, to Belfast. In them the tribal memory of 1641 lived on. They had been unaffected by the Enlightenment ferment of Belfast at the end of the previous century. This, along with Irish nationalism becoming Catholic nationalism, created unstable sectarian enclaves in a rapidly expanding industrialised Belfast.

Violence and political movements which exacerbated Protestant fears of being overwhelmed politically put more stress on alliances than they were capable of sustaining. A breakdown in Protestant/Catholic alliance took place later in the century, over support for the Land League. According to Jonathan Bardon, 'The danger of sectarian conflict was always there, but during most of 1880 and 1881 northern Protestants as well as Catholics thronged to attend league meetings and there was little violence . . .' When the 1881 Land Act was passed, it was greeted with acclaim in Ulster by tenants associations and Liberals. 'In the rest of Ireland the response to the act was mixed . . . violence raged over much of the south and during Parnell's imprisonment there were fourteen murders and sixty-one cases of 'firing at the person'. Ulster farmers, particularly Presbyterian members of tenants associations who had joined hands with the Land League, were deeply dismayed.[10]

Since most of the land in Ireland was owned by landlords, tenants were insecure. Under the 'Ulster Custom', tenants had been reimbursed for improvements which they had made. This had no force in law. The tenant right movement sought three Fs; fair rents, fixity of tenure and free sale of the tenant's interest in the holding.[11]

That movement was represented most significantly by the Reverend J.B. Armour of Ballymoney.[12] From his knowledge of the sufferings of his congregation, he had campaigned for tenant rights and pleaded with the Presbyterian Church to make common cause with its Catholic fellow-countrymen against its common enemy, the Anglican Ascendancy and the landowners. But the tenant right agenda was not the same as a nationalist agenda. Richard McMinn wrote of J.B. Armour:

> He was a complex character in a complex situation. His political career needs to be interpreted in the light of his aggressive Presbyterianism and his hostility towards the Anglican Church, the landed classes and the Conservative political establishment, the triform devil incarnate which he spent his life fighting. In that struggle the violent and unyielding nature of his language indicated the intensity of his feelings. Nowhere in his life is there any evidence of a positive feeling for the concept of Irish nationalism.[13]

REVIVAL AND REFORM IN THE CHURCHES IN THE 1800s

Two parallel things happened in the 1800s. There was a great strengthening of Presbyterianism through the experiences of the 1859 revival. A warmhearted evangelicalism became part of the life of the denomination and the position of lay people was greatly strengthened in the Church. An attempt was made to reach out to the Catholic people in evangelism.

At the same time the Irish Catholic Church was Romanised and reshaped under the leadership of Cardinal Paul Cullen and the ultramontanist movement. As Desmond Bowen has written in *Paul, Cardinal Cullen and the Shaping of Modern Irish Catholicism*: 'His task was clear, to put the Catholic Church in Ireland on a war footing against Protestantism and every other enemy of the Supreme Pontiff'.[14] In Finlay Holmes's words, 'As regards the future faith of the majority of Irish Roman Catholics, Cullen and Ultramontanism won. The Second Reformation, like the First, had failed in Ireland.'[15]

Two things occur to me at this point. One is Terence McCaughey's point that 'the story of confessional allegiance and the story of lost land became almost inextricably linked'.[16] The other point is one made by Finlay Holmes as to whether it is ever possible for a church associated with privilege to evangelise people who have been the direct losers in that equation. It is nevertheless important to recall that the Presbyterians were not part of the Ascendancy but were, like their Catholic neighbours, victims of it.

In the 1800s there developed strong religious communities. The Presbyterian one was evangelical and becoming increasingly unionist, especially after Home Rule became a possibility; the Anglicans took a similar line. At the same time, the newly disciplined Catholic Church, more Roman than it had been before, had an Irish nationalist orientation.

Protestant resistance to a united Ireland is often interpreted by nationalists as a defence of privilege. There is every reason why they should have seen the Protestant community as a privileged community. It would, however, be a mistake to interpret the reason for the resistance to a united Ireland as being mainly located in the concern to defend privilege. It was understood by Presbyterians as an issue of freedom and prosperity for the whole society.

The *Ne Temere* decree of 1907, which required that written undertakings be given that the children of mixed marriages be raised as Catholics, was the final push that tipped the waverers over to the unionist side. That decree persuaded them that Catholic ecclesiastical imperialism would predominate in a

Home Rule Ireland. On the eve of the General Election of 1910, eleven former Moderators of the General Assembly took the unusual step of publishing a manifesto in which they contended that the best interests of all the people of Ireland were safeguarded by the union with Great Britain.

A resolution was carried unanimously by the General Assembly in 1912 that:

> A separate parliament for Ireland . . . would, in our judgement, lead to the ascendancy of one class and creed in matters pertaining to religion, education and civil administration. We do not believe that any guarantees, moral or material, could be devised which could safeguard the rights and privileges of minorities scattered throughout Ireland against encroachment of a majority vested with legislative and executive functions.[17]

Raymond Helmick SJ gets to the heart of the distrust felt by the Protestant minority in Ireland as a whole which resisted Home Rule at that time. His analysis can be summarised as follows: 'The environment of clerical domination of Irish life and dread of that power led the Protestant people to look in the first instance, to defend the rights of dissenting non-conformist minorities. Being afraid of Rome rule they did not extend their hands generously to their Catholic neighbours, being afraid that if the dissenting tradition was not protected it would disappear in an environment which was centralist and authoritarian, or in one where the dissenting tradition would be consistently outvoted in a "democracy" which was intent on imposing policies at variance with dissenting notions of liberty.'[18]

AFTER PARTITION: WIDENING DIVISIONS

After Partition, the south of Ireland became a place where Catholic nationalism reigned supreme. For various and complex reasons, many Protestants emigrated and those who remained kept their heads down and made a living as private citizens.

Meanwhile, Northern Ireland was increasingly a place where people looked after their own and no one looked after everyone.

The relationships between the Protestant and Catholic Churches in Ireland were, by and large, in a frozen stalemate of animosity. In 1931, Cardinal MacRory declared that 'the Protestant Church in Ireland' was 'not even a part of the Church of Christ'. Many Protestants believed that the Catholic Church had a similar status; some still do. It is important for those of us who live on this side of Vatican II to take the trouble to think ourselves into the hostile attitudes which prevailed between the Churches, almost all over the world, before the 1960s.

Political and religious loyalties coalesced even further following Partition. Lord Craigavon declared that Northern Ireland was a Protestant state for a Protestant people. The members of the ruling Unionist Party had close associations with the Orange Order. De Valera's Ireland, in Seamus Heaney's words, was 'pastoral, pure and Papist'.[19]

Conor Cruise O'Brien writes about the close association between religion and the government in the south of Ireland as late as 1948:

> The new inter-party government . . . sent to the Vatican, from its first Cabinet meeting, the most effusively Catholic message ever sent by any Government of the Irish State, since its foundation in 1921. Their telegram desired 'to repose at the feet of your Holiness the assurance of our filial loyalty and of our devotion to your August Person, as well as our firm resolve to be guided in all our work by the teaching of Christ, and to strive for the attainment of a social order in Ireland based on Christian principles'. This was a Catholic–nationalist government with an unusually strong and explicit emphasis on the 'Catholic'.[20]

Many Presbyterians left the south. Those that stayed were encouraged by the General Assembly in 1922 'to co-operate wholeheartedly with their Roman Catholic fellow country-men in the best interests of their beloved land'. In 1924 the

Moderator of the Synod of Dublin, A.W. Neill, appealed to Presbyterians in the Free State: 'we must concentrate upon the business of building up our country's fortunes on sound lines . . . we must give our best in honesty, sincerity, yes, and in love'.[21]

Many Presbyterians regret that northern Catholics did not adopt a more positive attitude towards Northern Ireland. The written submission from the (Catholic) Irish Episcopal Conference to the New Ireland Forum in January 1984 reads:

> Widespread refusal to co-operate with the institutions of the new state was a marked feature of Catholic attitudes from the beginning . . . partly because they felt that non-cooperation would help to end a state which they regarded as non-viable, the Catholic community refused at first to work the institutions of Northern Ireland.[22]

This issue is explored in detail in a recently published Ph.D. thesis by Mary Harris.[23]

Cardinal Logue, the Catholic Archbishop of Armagh, could not see his way to attend the official opening of the Northern Ireland Parliament, which was boycotted for several years by its nationalist members.

One of the recurring anxieties for Presbyterians, making many of them resist a united Ireland, concerns the application of Catholic social teaching. Many years later, in 1980, the Catholic bishops of England and Wales wrote:

> We live in a society where many different moral and political opinions are conscientiously held and pursued in practice. We make no attempt to override the consciences of our fellow citizens. We do not seek to have Catholic moral teaching imposed by law, or even adopted as public policy. But we do have the right, as members of a pluralistic society, to appeal to the consciences not only of our fellow Catholics, but also of our fellow citizens and our political leaders and representatives.[24]

This seems perfectly reasonable, non-threatening and indeed

responsible when stated in a British context where there is a pluralistic society and the members of the Catholic Church are in a minority.

In their oral submission to the New Ireland Forum on 2 May 1984 the representatives of the Irish Episcopal Conference said:

> The Catholic Church in Ireland totally rejects the concept of a confessional state. We have not sought and we do not seek a Catholic State for a Catholic people. We believe that the alliance of Church and State is harmful for the Church and harmful for the State . . .
>
> We have repeatedly declared that we in no way seek to have the moral teaching of the Catholic Church become the criterion of constitutional change or to have the principles of Catholic faith enshrined in civil law. What we have claimed, and what we must claim, is the right to fulfil our pastoral duty and our pastoral duty is to alert the consciences of Catholics to the moral consequences of any proposed piece of legislation and the impact of that legislation on the moral quality of life in society while leaving to the legislators and to the electorate their freedom to act in accordance with their consciences.

While this statement is welcome, difficulties nevertheless arise in Ireland where the faithful membership of the Catholic Church is a majority of the population, and where a very significant proportion of that majority believes that the moral opinions voiced by the teaching authority are expressions of a moral order which are for the good of society and ought to be enshrined in legislation or even in the Constitution. When tested in a referendum, these opinions may express the democratic wish of the majority, but may take insufficient account of the rights and wishes of a minority.

De facto coalitions of unionism with Protestantism and Catholicism with nationalism became consolidated. I know of one Presbyterian minister, who on going to a new congregation was invited automatically by the local Unionist Association to be its chairman. On the nationalist side, Eamonn McCann wrote of how 'the party was closely associated with the Catholic Church. Its basic unit of organisation was not the electoral ward but the parish . . . Nationalist candidates were not selected; they were anointed.'[25]

Following Partition, much was achieved materially within Northern Ireland, while at the same time relationships between north and south and between nationalists and unionists deteriorated. The border was the prior question at all times.

Issues of social justice and community reconciliation were forgotten. The unionist people were largely unaware that there was increasing anger within the nationalist community concerning discrimination and inequality, accompanied by unionist unwillingness to recognise and honour Irish cultural identity. Those Catholic complaints which did filter through to Protestant consciousness were widely perceived as the expression of a carefully nurtured sense of grievance which, they believed, 'finds imaginary grounds where real ones do not exist and exaggerates them greatly where they do'.[26] It would be difficult to imagine two groups of people living so close together and failing so completely either to understand or to accommodate one another.

FINDING THE TRUTH

After what many in the Protestant community saw as fifty years of progress, made in the face of constant hostility from the Republic of Ireland and less than whole-hearted co-operation from their nationalist fellow-citizens in Northern Ireland, it came as a considerable shock for them to be vilified in 1968 before world opinion as a discriminating gang of bigots. It continues to rankle that the nationalist interpretation of reality, which seems unwilling to acknowledge that it made any negative contribution to the difficulties, appears to have won the propaganda battle. It has driven Protestants deeper into self-righteousness and isolation. It has to be said that Presbyterians had not rocked the unionist boat in the interests of their Catholic neighbours. Indeed, such was the gulf in understanding and communication between the two groups, that that would have been unlikely, however desirable.

Nevertheless, after Vatican II, Presbyterians thought that relationships were improving and welcomed the change. Prior to 1968 there was some indication that the Presbyterian Church was trying to get beyond the propaganda to the truth.

As early as 1965, the General Assembly urged:

> upon our people humbly and frankly to acknowledge and to ask forgiveness for any attitudes and actions towards our Roman Catholic fellow-countrymen which have been unworthy of our calling as followers of Jesus Christ; and that the Assembly call upon our people to resolve to deal with all conflicts of interest, loyalties, or beliefs always in the spirit of charity rather than of suspicion and intolerance and in accordance with the truth set out in scripture.

A 1967 pre-Troubles report to the General Assembly on 'Religious Discrimination in Ireland' welcomed:

> a gradual easing of tension and an improvement in relationships between the various groups in Ireland. Slowly, suspicion, bigotry and intolerance have subsided; and although co-operation among people of different religious and political persuasions is still very limited in some places, it is gradually increasing year by year. So far as specifically religious attitudes are concerned, the short reign of Pope John XXIII undoubtedly brought about a warmer climate in ecclesiastical affairs and has encouraged the growth of a friendlier spirit on nearly all sides.[27]

That report also called for fair employment, for promotion on merit and a points system for the allocation of housing. The 1967 report represents a serious attempt by Presbyterians to engage in a process of constructive critical reflection. Those were years of hope which were dashed in the events which were to follow so soon after.

It is a pity that the short period of hope between 1965 and 1968 could not have been developed into a constructive process across the political spectrum which would have led to significant peaceful change. We often fail to appreciate that reform in the direction of justice strengthens a society.

Presbyterian reflective thought on these issues was matched by similar moves in other directions. The Catholic Bishop of Down and Connor, William Philbin, accepted an invitation to a reception in Belfast City Hall; the Nationalist MP Eddie McAteer addressed Young Unionists at Queen's University; in 1963 Young Unionists went to Dublin for talks with Fine Gael, and the Union Jack was flown at half mast on the City Hall as a mark of respect on the death of Pope John XXIII.[28]

Those people who resisted necessary reform and those who fomented discord in a volatile situation carry a heavy weight of responsibility for detonating twenty-five years of mayhem. People who chose not to handle the volatile and potentially explosive situation with care put themselves and thousands of others at risk.

The descent into communal disorder and violence could be described as the struggles of people locked in ideological conflicts of a most basic and elemental kind who had not found an adequate way of communicating constructively with one another.

Once the Cameron Report on the 1968 disturbances was published,[29] and some dialogue began across the lines of rupture, some Presbyterians began to understand that Catholic grievances about gerrymandering and other issues were not imaginary, but had a foundation in more than political propaganda. Since that time the Presbyterian Church has analysed the issues on a continuing basis and has supported policies aimed at addressing issues of fairness and justice and the accommodation of diversity.

The most recent comprehensive analysis was the 1993 report to the General Assembly 'Presbyterian principles and political witness' which acknowledges that:

The Presbyterian Church shares the guilt of the majority community in Northern Ireland for tolerating the practice of discrimination in jobs, housing and voting rights which largely led to the Civil Rights Campaign of the 1960s.[30]

While hindsight does not confer moral superiority, it is nevertheless regrettable that there was neither sufficient grace nor political will to offer generosity across these divisions when it was required. The whole community failed, in 1968 and thereafter, to come together to understand one another and to address the outstanding issues together.

On the important issue of fair employment the Presbyterian Church has expressed full support for fair employment practices. The General Assembly Minutes of 1976 record:

> that the General Assembly welcomes enactment of legislation designed to eliminate unjust discrimination in the selection, retention and dismissal of employees on the grounds of race, colour, sex, marital status, religion, political opinion, national extraction or social origin.

It is often difficult to see through what may be interpreted as party political considerations to the question of justice at the heart of some of these issues.

Catholic disadvantage in the job market is a complex matter and is not amenable either to simple explanation or to simple solutions. One of the most helpful reports on this subject was issued by the Presbyterian Church USA.

> A persistent pattern of Protestant domination in higher echelons of management, in skilled jobs, and in old, established industries with the highest wages characterises the situation. While examples of Catholic discrimination against Protestants do exist, and Catholics do hold positions in certain industries out of proportion to their numbers in the work force, the reverse is more often the case . . .
>
> Discrimination is not the sole cause of the problem. Ireland's tortured history, with Catholic pitted against Protestant, Irish

against English, and rich against poor has bred a legacy of strife with few parallels. Sectarian divisions begat segregated living patterns. Entrepreneurs located their businesses to draw exclusively from Protestant or Catholic neighbourhoods. Workers secured housing adjacent to factories with sectarian hiring policies. The fear of crossing through hostile neighbourhoods chilled efforts to gain employment across sectarian lines. Jobs were a family affair, and information about them passed by word of mouth. A segregated school system with Catholics stressing liberal arts and Protestants the practical and technical arts combined with the other factors to give advantage to Protestants in the technology-based basic industries of Northern Ireland and to relegate Catholics to semi- and unskilled jobs.

In all this Protestants tended to emerge as 'winners' . . .

In the present day discrimination is exacerbated by the decline of basic industries, lack of new investment and continuing violence.[31]

Catholic men are 2.1 times more likely to be unemployed than Protestant men; Catholic women 1.5 times more likely than Protestant women. Catholic male unemployment stands at 23 per cent and Protestant male unemployment at 11 per cent. The comparable figures for women are 11 per cent and 7 per cent. There are serious disparities within particular industries and the really difficult problems lie in the areas of urban deprivation and unemployment.

Northern Ireland needs more jobs and a full commitment to strong fair employment laws. The initiative taken in January 1994 by the four largest Churches in Ireland and their counterparts in the United States in 'The call for fair employment and investment' was an important attempt to provide 'common ground where religious leaders and other people of good will can agree to work together on these matters.'[32]

This issue is increasingly being seen as an issue of justice. It is an instance where legislation on matters like fair employment can force people to face up to issues and, in the process, learn to look beyond the packaging to the core concern. This learning process has been seriously impeded by the violence and the anger and suspicion engendered by it. Now that the violence has stopped, hopefully we can make more progress on these fronts.

Over the period of the Troubles, the Presbyterian Church has been supportive of the Royal Ulster Constabulary, believing that the job was by and large well done in a very difficult situation. The security forces had a thankless and dangerous job to do and much of the criticism of them seemed to take insufficient account of the fact that nearly five hundred local people serving in the security forces had been killed and nearly eight thousand had been injured. They were regularly engaged in very dangerous situations and protected the whole community from the worst ravages of ruthless and efficient terrorist organisations. Many had to leave their homes and relocate their families in less vulnerable areas. Many members of the General Assembly who were discussing these issues and were passing resolutions had buried members of their congregations who served in the security forces and were still caring for their bereaved families. Any criticism of the security forces was offered seriously but quietly, rather than shouted from the housetops.

In 1990 the Assembly passed a resolution expressing 'appreciation for the protection offered by the security forces in Northern Ireland and in the Republic of Ireland', but the Assembly also affirmed 'that only the highest standards on the part of the Security Forces is acceptable', and recognised 'that alleged cases of unprofessional behaviour must be investigated and the guilty brought to justice'. This kind of resolution represents a warning that the Church expects high standards in this area of life.

Some Presbyterians were shocked to hear of the allegations made against the police in the case of the UDR Four. Protests by the nationalist community had tended to be treated with some suspicion, on the grounds that they might have been politically motivated. After the UDR Four case, people wondered if unacceptable methods were being used to extract confessions from suspects. The Assembly has recognised the complexity of many of these cases, and while individual Presbyterians have been involved in particular campaigns, the Church has acted with caution, being reluctant to adopt a campaigning position on any of them.

Statements issued by the General Assembly reflect the convictions of the members of the Assembly. Since they are not used normally as campaigning documents, there is always the danger that they remain as words on a page. Sometimes they are disseminated to a wider audience as when documents are sent for study and comment to presbyteries and kirk sessions. The issues may be included in sermons and in pulpit announcements. The 'Mission Statement' of the 1992 Assembly and the 1994 'Peace Vocation' have both been widely circulated, commended and taught throughout the Church. One of the most effective ways for the convictions of the Church to reach a wider audience is through the Moderator's availability to the media.

While the Presbyterian Church has pointed the way towards the need for political compromise and accommodation, it has not attempted to devise a particular political model through which this might be done nor have its resolutions always reflected the opinions of the wider Protestant community.

Perhaps the clearest linkage between Protestantism and the political system has been the Orange Order. Many Protestants in Northern Ireland have been influenced by the perspectives of the Order. This linkage makes it difficult for them to separate loyalty to Jesus Christ from loyalty to the Crown and Constitution. The Orange Order, with its associations between Protestantism and unionism, provides the model of interpretation for a community's experiences.

There is no formal link between the Presbyterian Church and the Orange Order. Members of the Church make up their own minds whether to belong or not. Kirk sessions may grant the use of churches to the Order from time to time for services of worship. This is a local decision and the choice of the preacher lies with the local minister.

There was much dismay in 1992 at the activities of some people associated with Orange lodges, who behaved in an outrageous way in the Lower Ormeau Road following the earlier loyalist attack on a bookmaker's shop. I was of the opinion that if the march was passing along that stretch of road, the members of the Order ought to have walked in silence out of respect for the dead and the sensitivities of local people. I know many people within the Order are annoyed at the macho attitudes of some of the 'Kick the Pope' flute bands. Since they get the Orange Order a bad name, the Order would do well to control them or dispense with their services altogether.

As far as my own Church is concerned, it seems to me that we have failed in the following ways:

we have been taken over by the siege mentality to such a degree that we have lost our spiritual freedom in Christ;

we have not been able to appreciate the culture and history of the people with whom we share this island and we have thereby impoverished ourselves;

we have not understood that the other side of the Battle of the Boyne has been a history of dispossession and humiliation for our neighbours and we do not seem to see that you cannot love your neighbour and celebrate his defeat, at one and the same time;

we have not understood that the Catholic community in Northern Ireland feels threatened by the weight of a unionist majority backed by the weight of Britain;

Protestantism frequently presents itself with an intolerant and arrogant face.

Our Churches have to struggle to escape from being imprisoned within the perspectives of alienated communities. We find it difficult to provide the prophetic, critical and visionary insight which is often required. This failure has serious consequences both for the Church and for politics. If we provide an uncritical chaplaincy service to political ideologies we confer a quasi-religious character upon them. Necessary political compromise can then be portrayed as the betrayal of a religious trust. Politics need to be desacralised so that they become manageable and in the process the Churches will be set free to be the Church.

5

A PRECARIOUS BELONGING

THE FAULTED LEDGE

In his poem 'Conacre', John Hewitt, in hoping that the time might come when he would 'find this nation' as his own, described it in the meantime as a 'faulted ledge'. It bespeaks a precarious existence.

The precarious belonging was an early experience. Having encountered the lack of hospitality of Thomas Wentworth, Charles I's lord deputy, some Presbyterians tried to leave shortly after they had arrived. Principal Davey wrote of an early attempt to transplant themselves to more hospitable shores.

> On 9th September, 1636, a small sailing vessel of one hundred and fifty tons, built at Groomsport, set out from Belfast Lough with the intention of reaching New England. On board this vessel named Eagle Wing in hope of a speedy crossing were one hundred and forty Presbyterians of Northern Ireland, including such leaders of the Church in those days as Blair, Hamilton and Livingstone. After weathering one storm which drove them to shelter, they made a fresh beginning and were already more than half-way across the Atlantic when a new and frightful tempest struck them, and after a valiant and persevering attempt to hold on their course, they were forced to turn for home with broken

rudder, torn sails, leaking sides, and ripped up decks; and by November they were back again at Carrickfergus . . .

Like good colonists they took the failure of their enterprise to indicate the will of God that they should not further emulate the Pilgrim Fathers, but should stay and do His work in Ireland.[1]

The next exodus, this time to Scotland and the islands, took place during the 1641 rebellion. That was followed, towards the end of the century, by journeys to places further afield. No legal right to establish alternative Church structures to the Established Church existed in Ireland. Bishop Jeremy Taylor in a single day deprived thirty-six Presbyterian ministers of their liberty to preach. Francis Makemie, who became the father of Presbyterianism in America, was ordained in 1682 by the Laggan presbytery for service in Maryland in response to an appeal for Presbyterian ministers for that colony.[2]

More departures followed in the next century, maybe as many as 250,000. With the famines of the early 1700s which may have been responsible for the deaths of 300,000 people and the raising of rents and tithes of those who had improved their holdings, America seemed to be a very attractive place in terms of liberty, opportunity and available land.[3]

The 1800s saw the consolidation of Presbyterianism, both in the number of congregations established and, as a consequence of the 1859 revival, in the fervour and commitment of the people. There was a doctrinal unity within the new General Assembly and Presbyterians 'were finding an increasingly recognised place in society'.[4]

The Presbyterian population reached its historic maximum of 642,000 people in 1834, 8.1 per cent of Ireland's population. While the intervening years have seen both very significant decreases in the total number of Presbyterians in Ireland and significant shifts in their location, their percentage of the overall population has remained remarkably steady. By 1901 the numbers had fallen to 443,000, 9.9 per cent of the total. In 1971 it was 422,000, 9.3 per cent of the total. Clearly, while the experience of Presbyterians has in many places been that of a precarious belonging, resulting in emigration and relocation, the overall disastrous outflow of people from Ireland has meant that Presbyterians remain as a steady percentage of the whole.[5]

DEMOGRAPHIC SHIFTS OF POPULATION THIS CENTURY

Following the upheavals of the Anglo-Irish War of 1919–21 and the Civil War, Presbyterian numbers in the south of Ireland fell sharply. Principal John M. Barkley wrote:

> by March 31 1922, by murder, burnings-out and terrorism, Presbyterian numbers had been reduced in the presbytery of Athlone by 30 per cent, of Connaught by 36 per cent, of Cork by 45 per cent, of Dublin by 16 per cent and of Munster by 44 per cent – not to mention their dead, and the destruction in the nine counties of Ulster.[6]

Over the years there has been a steady haemorrhaging of the Presbyterian population from the Republic of Ireland. Some of it was due to the exodus of those who worked in the various elements of the British administration; some to the Catholic Church's policy on mixed marriages; some of it by Presbyterian families coming north; some of it to the high emigration rates across the board from the south, suffered by the overall population. On the migration issue, Garret FitzGerald maintains that the Protestants were less affected than the rest of the population.

The *Ne Temere* decree destroyed the old custom of the sons of mixed marriages going to church with the father and the daughters with the mother.

> Marrying a Catholic was taboo. Many Protestants in country areas preferred to die alone. Even in the '60s just over half of the Protestant women of marriagable age found a partner and two out of every three Protestant men were bachelors. It seemed that the southern Irish Protestant was in danger of extinction.[7]

William Trevor's novels and short stories about the decline of Protestant families in the south make moving but profoundly depressing reading.

So depressing was the outlook within Presbyterianism that Dr Trevor Morrow, the minister of Lucan Church, Co. Dublin, recently described the Church growth policy of the Presbyterian Church in the south as a 'Mortuary Model': growth was hardly expected; congregations were serviced with the ordinances of religion and the people provided with ministers until the members died and the congregations were closed and the buildings sold off as libraries or whatever. Survival was the most that could be expected.

In the last ten years there has been a change for the better. If the violence has ended and we can arrive at an acceptable political settlement, then the Presbyterian Church faces a moment of opportunity, provided it is committed to building relationships of trust and friendship with people across the ancient lines of bitterness and mistrust.

Since I have never worked in the Republic I have talked to people who have lived there, most of them all their lives. I am interested to know what is happening to Presbyterians in that society. In 1920 there were approximately 50,000 Presbyterians in what was to become the Republic of Ireland.[8] In 1993 the number was 13,227.[9]

CORK PRESBYTERIANS

Trinity Presbyterian Church in Cork is a large spacious building capable of seating about five hundred people. The average attendance on Sunday, at present, is about forty, consisting of thirty adults and ten children. Like many another Presbyterian Church in the Republic of Ireland, it speaks eloquently of what used to be and evidences the contemporary struggle of a Presbyterian community to survive.

On the wall of the church there is a memorial listing the names of forty-eight members who served in the 1914–18 war and of an additional nine who died. There is now no family name on the memorial tablet still represented in the membership of the congregation, although some of the families still exist in Cork, having 'married out' to Catholics or Anglicans. It does not take too much effort to imagine the traumatic nature of the change for the Cork congregation when, on the one hand, they remembered those who were killed and served in the 1914–18 war, and on the other hand found themselves three years later no longer a part of the country which those people had served. As Dr Barkley indicated, by March 1922 the Presbyterian numbers in the presbytery of Cork had fallen by 45 per cent.

Presbyterian numbers in Cork had peaked in 1911 with 236 families in two congregations. The reduction in the size of the Presbyterian community in Cork was such that the two Presbyterian congregations of Trinity and Queen Street united in 1928 with a total membership of 155 families.

DUBLIN PRESBYTERIANS

Dublin is quite different from Cork, partly due to the greater number of members. As with Cork, many Dublin Presbyterians have no connection with the Plantation. They came as business people or as engineers from the Scottish universities. South of a line between Dublin and Sligo, Presbyterian roots lie primarily in the world of industry and commerce. Those who stayed after Independence were committed to Ireland and kept their money in the country. Some, connected with British administration, left. Rathgar congregation in south Dublin may have lost about two hundred families at that time.

Some Rathgar Presbyterians told me that in the eyes of most Catholics, Presbyterian identity is not differentiated within the wider Protestant identity. When Presbyterians identify themselves as such, most people are unsure as to what is meant.

Remembrance Sunday is still observed in Rathgar Church in November each year, since members served in both World Wars. The British national anthem was used until about 1947. The minute's silence is still observed and a wreath laid, but the remembrance now includes all those killed in war and not specifically in the two World Wars.

With time, there has come an increasing awareness of being Irish. As far as identity is concerned, some Dublin Presbyterians told me that it is not thought possible to be both British and Irish. Younger Dublin Presbyterians love their country. It is where they were born and where they live. Presbyterians in the north are a mystery to them. It is right that Presbyterianism in Ireland in general, and in the Republic in particular, must be more than a 'Scots-Irish' Church if people from an Irish Catholic background are ever to think of joining it. If it is possible to be an Irish-American in America, is it possible to be Scots-Irish in Dublin, or does that make you second-class Irish?

There is some apprehension now because of falling numbers. Evangelism has not been easy. Secular Ireland may provide more space for this than a Catholic Ireland. In one area of Dublin, where less than 10 per cent of the population go to any church, it is said that encouragement was given by the local priests to the Methodists to do what they could to reach people.

Thirty-five of the families in Rathgar Church are interchurch families. Such families tend to go with the parent of stronger faith. As the Catholic Church loses some of its influence, some Catholics choose the Presbyterian tradition because of its emphasis on the rights of conscience of the individual. They are against being told what to do and they also like the democracy within the Presbyterian Church.

The conversations with Presbyterians in Dublin indicate a shift of identity, an accommodation to the new reality. Their unease with the more strident voices of unionism and sometimes with what they maintain are insensitive and unhelpful Presbyterian statements coming out of Belfast, indicate both an embarrassment and an almost total lack of sympathy for the way things are expressed 'up there'. Presbyterian young adults from Dublin have an explicit Irish identity with no overtones of special affection for northern unionists or for Britain.

COUNTY DONEGAL PRESBYTERIANS

One gets the impression that Donegal Presbyterians are a cohesive and confident people, at peace with themselves and their neighbours in a county marked by general warmth, togetherness and compassion.

There are 34 Presbyterian congregations with 1,867 families comprising a stable community of over 5,844 people. Like the Presbyterians in Dublin, some of them feel somewhat of a minority within the denomination, comprised as it is mostly of people from Northern Ireland. Nearly all look upon Dublin as their political and national capital, and while having a sense of empathy with their Protestant co-religionists in Northern Ireland who have suffered from IRA violence, some of it emanating from Donegal, they have little sense of empathy with Unionist politicians. They vote mainly for Labour and Fine Gael. Donegal Orangeism has a strong sense of belonging to east Donegal. As one Orangeman said on RTE, he is 'happy to be Irish, with different roots: proud to be Protestant'. The sense of Irish identity increases with distance from the border and every generation; the older people resenting the fact that they were abandoned, some might say betrayed, by the six counties at the time of Partition.

Donegal Presbyterians share the wider Irish culture of hospitality, enjoying the freedom to develop Irish music and dancing. Donegal tends to be anti-authoritarian: for example, celebrating their sense of local identity and their distance from Dublin, local people tend to take their own decisions on issues like planning.

There is an automatic church-going tradition among the

people of Donegal which provides an overall spiritual background to life which is very different from the arid godlessness of much of contemporary England.

KILKENNY PRESBYTERIANS

The Presbyterian Church almost died in Kilkenny in the 1950s when the congregation was reduced to four people. They struggled on with faith and prayer and a few other people joined them. By the 1980s it had grown to fifteen families comprising about thirty people.

Some remarkable things have happened recently. There is now in 1995 a congregation of about three hundred people who have come from all kinds of Church backgrounds and found a comfortable spiritual home within a welcoming church community. A new church has been built to accommodate the congregation. Very few people from Northern Ireland belong to the congregation, therefore they all have an Irish identity. Since most of them do not come from a Presbyterian background they may have a Presbyterian identity problem.

Like many another Presbyterian church in the Republic it suffers from geographic isolation from other Presbyterian churches. This congregation seeks to maintain open and warmhearted relationships with all the other Churches in the town. They have as much 'space' as they need to live and worship as they wish.

SUPPRESSED MEMORY OR ACCOMMODATION?

These brief case studies demonstrate both the diversity of situations found in the Republic of Ireland and the changing situation.

David Stevens, the General Secretary of the Irish Council of Churches, has written about the way Protestants in the Republic have dealt with adjustment and a possible suppression of memory.

The Southern Protestant tradition since the middle of the nine-teenth century can, I believe, be understood as one of pain, despair, disdain, withdrawal, uneasy belonging, and, finally, a suppression of memory. These feelings are part of the explana-tion for the well-nigh terminal spinelessness that afflicted the Southern Protestant community until recently . . .

Has the pain of change led to the suppression of memory or even to an obliteration of memory? Has this in fact been the price of change? Or have the memories gone because they are no longer relevant, because the antagonisms have disappeared, because the ambiguity of the Protestant position in Ireland – at least in the South – has been resolved? [10]

Dr Stevens raises questions to which I do not know the answer. I get the impression that Protestantism in the Republic has become, in some places, a private domesticated affair, but that is changing.

When I asked some Presbyterians in a congregation in the Republic near the border if they were Irish, I found only one person prepared to say 'yes' without qualification. Some of them had family members living in dangerous areas in Northern Ireland and would have had sympathy with the unionist posi-tion. The general sentiment was: 'You can get on all right down here if you keep your mouth shut.' While I was assured that this may be a characteristic of some areas near the border, it would not be true of Presbyterian churches further away from it.

At a local level throughout the country there is marked co-operation across the Church divisions. Protestants speak regularly of the generous help given to them by their Catholic neighbours at events organised to raise money to assist them in keeping the church buildings open.

One wonders why some southern Presbyterians are reluctant to get into debates on public issues and why, for instance, there is only one Presbyterian TD in the Dáil. Is it because they would be thought to be disloyal, wanting to impose Protestant liberal values on a Catholic people? Would some Catholic people say,

'It's none of their business' or 'They have no morals anyway'?
  Victor Griffen, one time Dean of St Patrick's Cathedral in
Dublin, and one who tended not to follow the pattern of keep-
ing his mouth shut, said of southern Protestants:

> They gave the impression of being happy because they offered no
> word of criticism. Nevertheless they felt alienated within a Gaelic
> Nationalist Roman Catholic State. They were in the State but did
> not in all things belong.[11]

'In but not of' the state maybe, but nevertheless Herbert Butler's
remark that 'the home of the heart and the mind was always in
this country'[12] indicates a deeper sense of belonging to the
country, as distinct from the state.

THE MOVEMENT OF PRESBYTERIANS WITHIN NORTHERN IRELAND

The last twenty-five years of violence has had a very significant
effect upon many Presbyterian congregations.

DERRY

People keep telling me that Derry is different from the rest of Northern Ireland. I am told this is partly due to the size of the city
and to a strong sense of local identity. This is the city which was
traumatised by the killing of thirteen demonstrators by the army
in January 1972. I have neither lived nor worked there, so I went
to find out what has happened to the Presbyterians since 1968.

Strand Church

In 1968 Strand Church on the city side was on the crest of a wave;
full of confidence and hope, with a packed church for Sunday
worship. Their much-loved and respected minister Dr Montgomery had retired and a new minister, the Reverend Maurice
Bolton, had been installed.

The intervening years have been a story of courage, struggle and disappointment. The congregational size has fallen from 500 families to 182. A member of the congregation, RUC Inspector Norman Duddy, was murdered by the IRA in the street outside the church after the morning service in March 1982. While this brought the people closer together, it profoundly shocked the congregation.

One has to understand the nature of a Presbyterian congregation in a place like Derry. It does not consist of a group of strangers who gather on a Sunday for worship, thereafter to scatter. A congregation is a closely knit unit of service and fellowship; with congregational life packed with organisations run by the members; the leaders and the committee are elected by the people and the minister has been called by the people. It is difficult to quantify the effect upon such a fellowship when one of their number is efficiently targeted and murdered outside the church after a service. Such an attack is experienced as an attack upon the church community as a whole as well as an attack upon an individual. People stand by stunned and powerless; a triumph of savagery.

Carlisle Road

When the Reverend Richard Graham came to Carlisle Road, again on the city side of the River Foyle, in 1965, it was to a thriving congregation of four hundred families. It was possible for him to do nearly all of his pastoral work by walking round the parish, for most of the people lived around the church. By 1994 the congregation was reduced to 280 families with only 50 remaining on the city side; the rest have moved across the river to the Waterside. Those who have remained on the city side are mainly elderly. The Sunday School has been reduced from 240 to 80 children. Like Strand Church, it is an aging congregation with few children and increasing leadership problems.

The reduction in the size of the congregations is paralleled in what happened to the overall Protestant population on the city side of the river, which fell from 18,000 in 1968 to 2,800 in 1994. Between 1968 and 1994 13,000 Protestants left the city side; another 2,100 were lost through natural death.

Paul Sweeney, a Derry Catholic, spoke of growing up

> in a working-class Catholic–Protestant community in Derry which was virtually fifty-fifty. Materially there was very little to choose between the two traditions. However, I was accustomed to a perceived natural order i.e. the Protestants were in ascendancy and we were in a state of slightly lesser beings . . .
>
> The late 60s witnessed a wind of change in the City . . . By '74 nobody seemed to have noticed that up to 10,000 Protestants had left the Derry side to live in the Waterside. The big question later became 'WERE THEY PUSHED OR DID THEY JUMP?' This subject matter was recently explored in a TV production 'A River Crossing' in which Dr Anthony Clare examined this Protestant migration. The programme testifies to the real fears of the Protestant community. The Catholic community rationalised this movement as voluntary apartheid on the part of their former Protestant neighbours, who had decided that they did not want to share that part of the world as equals.[13]

What do the Presbyterians have to say about it?

From 1968–71 some people chose to move to new developments on the Waterside; not because of intimidation at this stage. In the redevelopment of the Protestant Fountain area, fewer houses were built than had previously stood there, and so the population fell. Once the serious troubles started, the environment became unpleasant. Many Protestants left the Culmore owner-occupied area: some were connected with the security forces and it was an unsafe place for them to live. Before the new Foyle Bridge was built, it was experienced as an isolated area, since the only way out and into the rest of Northern Ireland was into and through the city and across the Craigavon Bridge.

Once people in the Protestant communities on the city side

became uncertain, it only took one case of intimidation or murder to destabilise a wide circle of people. Many who were bombed or burned out of businesses fought back into business time and again, only to be intimidated, targeted and bombed again. Many became discouraged and frustrated. They watched the security forces unable to protect their lives and property. The heart was knocked out of many people when the bombing and burnings were accompanied with assassinations of their friends.

I was told quite firmly that the Protestants who had left would never return to live on the city side in any numbers. After the Protestant Fountain area within the city is redeveloped again this year, some people will come back to that area, but not into the adjoining areas where large numbers of Protestants once lived.

Did the Presbyterians agree with what was going on before 1968? Was the gerrymandering of the electoral boundaries deemed not to be a matter for Christian conscience? If a minister raised the issue in a sermon would it inevitably have caused trouble between himself and the congregation? Would such trouble be thought to have needlessly impaired the warmth of his relationships with the people and have damaged the effectiveness of his ministry? If it was inappropriate to deal with the matter in the pulpit, where could it be dealt with? If it was thought to be too political to mention from the pulpit, would the presbytery have been an appropriate place to discuss the issues? Would the church have been a willing partner in seeing a shift in the control of the Londonderry Corporation from the unionists to the nationalists?

The situation throws up an interesting series of questions.

Not only were the city's electoral boundaries gerrymandered, houses were built and rented to consolidate unionist political power. Efforts to have a non-unionist deputy mayor came to nothing. The Presbyterian Church did not necessarily agree with this, but said little.

I came across this story about a highly principled Derry Presbyterian elder of integrity and scrupulous honesty. During the troubles of the early part of this century he lived with his family in Donegal, later moving to Derry where he eventually settled. In the 1970s, when he was quite an old man, he suffered a serious illness, during one night of which he became very agitated and distressed. Upon his recovery his son asked him what had been going through his mind. He was at first reluctant to talk about it, but eventually admitted that he had been re-living an incident of his teenage years in Donegal.

He had been a witness to an attempt by armed republicans to carry out a violent foray which had been frustrated. Later they came for him; he was convinced they meant to kill him. He managed to escape from them when they were surprised by a police patrol. His entire family, however, lived under threat and soon afterwards left Donegal for good. Not wanting to burden his children with the story and its implications, he had kept it to himself, where its terror was lodged deep within his memory.

This man had often expressed his dislike of many of the policies and attitudes of Derry's unionist administrations. Indeed at times he held them in contempt. But he always voted for them. His son asked him how he could do this, especially since he professed a strong evangelical Christian faith. Was it honest to support people for whom he had little respect? This is what he replied: 'There is nothing in my Bible that tells me that I should either like or respect the party I vote for; but they have erected a wall at my back which has protected me from people who once tried to kill me.'

This man had a business in the city side of Derry. The IRA intimidated him and finally bombed him out of his business, while he stood in the street and watched what he had worked for go up in flames. Those who tried to kill him in Donegal, burned him out of his business nearly sixty years later. At no time did he have any formal connection to a political party.

This is what the Protestant siege mentality is about and why perhaps the Church did so little.

It is right to commend the present Derry City Council, who are now assiduously trying to build bridges of understanding and promote the recognition of the importance of the culture and history of both communities. The trouble is that most of the Protestants have now left.

NEWRY

Newry is my home town. It always had a Protestant minority. Like Northern Ireland as a whole, it was a place where everyone looked after their own and no one looked after everybody. Discrimination was practised in both directions.

Newry has suffered from a high degree of IRA violence. While the IRA has been accused of bombing Catholic business places in Newry when the owners would not pay protection money, the main focus of their violence, particularly in the early years of the Troubles, was Protestant-owned businesses.

What has happened in the town has affected the churches. My home congregation of Sandy's Street in Newry is very much smaller than it was in 1968. The number of families has fallen from 240 to 151; the total number of persons in the congregation from a total of 810 to 395 individuals; the number of children from 193 to 58. My old primary school, the Model School, which used to have an enrolment of 380, is likely to close in 1995, the numbers having fallen to 33, of whom only 11 are Protestants. That will leave one 'controlled', that is, Protestant, primary school in the town where once there were two. The enrolment of the one which will survive is 225 compared to a pre-Troubles enrolment of 309. The total primary school population in the non-Catholic sector has fallen from 689 to 258. Those who are left feel increasingly isolated. For example, in youth work it is not possible to do the kind of work with a dozen young people that used to be done with sixty.

Why have Presbyterians moved from the town?

One man, who moved to Banbridge, did so because his son who was in the RAF was not able to stay in the house while he was on leave because it was too dangerous.

When I asked another young man why he was no longer living in the town in which he was raised, he put it down to a number of factors. He has attended about twenty-four funerals of people murdered by the IRA, one of them murdered in the car immediately behind the one he was driving home from work. He wants his young children raised in a stable environment where they could gain much from vibrant church and community activities which are no longer available, as they once were, to the Protestant community in Newry.

When I asked another couple why they had moved they said that their determination to remain in Newry was eventually worn down by the bombings and the murder of people they knew, some of them their friends, along with an accumulation of small things. Their quality of life gradually went, diminished with constant trouble like getting the car tyres slashed; the car windows broken; the fence daubed with paint; being on guard duty at the church during services in case it was bombed. They described their move to Banbridge as a move away from constant anxiety and fear to peace of mind. They experienced life in Newry as being part of a community under siege. They thought that it was unlikely that Protestants who had moved would ever return.

The council, which has an SDLP majority, has made serious efforts to build relationships and the Unionists have responded, but one gets the impression that the violence has done an enormous amount of damage to relationships which will be very difficult to repair.

BELFAST

The overall population of Belfast has been falling, but the percentage fall of Presbyterian numbers has been even more rapid. Between 1967 and 1987 the number of Presbyterian families in the synod of Belfast fell by 34 per cent and the number of Presbyterian persons by 46 per cent. The Sunday School enrolment fell by 68 per cent and the number of baptisms by 71 per cent. Belfast used to be a Presbyterian city. Not any more. It may soon have a nationalist majority on the council.

North Belfast, where I work, was described in 1955 by the then Moderator of the General Assembly and minister of Fortwilliam Park Church, as the 'most Presbyterian part of the city'. The North Belfast presbytery is currently engaged upon a study to see how the number of congregations can be adjusted to cope with the fall in numbers as the Catholic percentage of the population increases.

Many Presbyterians have moved from the city to the surrounding towns. As the Malone, Antrim and Upper Ormeau roads become increasingly Catholic, there seems to be a regrettable reluctance on the part of middle-class Presbyterians to buy houses in those areas, even though the physical and social environment is excellent, with good schools and churches. Perhaps with the end to violence people will once again welcome the opportunity to live in mixed areas and will prefer that to living in homogeneous communities.

While Presbyterians have been aware of the effects of the Troubles on the Church population, the other challenge of increasing secularisation has been given less attention than it deserves. Presbyterians have traditionally been anxious about the effects of Catholicism, but this other influence has been eating away at the heart of the Church. This is particularly true in the urban areas.

HOMOGENEOUS COMMUNITIES

The Presbyterian congregations of north Antrim remain strong. There are large and small congregations in that area which have been there for generations. The commitment and enthusiasm of the people are admirable and there seems to be nothing in terms of building and repairs that they are not prepared to attempt. In many ways these congregations represent something of the strength of Presbyterianism. Their situation is less precarious than some others, but their isolation from much of the immediate effects of the Troubles may give them a very inadequate grasp of the precarious nature of the existence of their fellow Presbyterians in other parts of the country.

Congregations in some parts of Northern Ireland are coping with falling numbers, wondering how to manage retraction, while others are growing. The presbyteries rejoicing in larger numbers need to beware that they are not living in a fool's paradise. What they are benefiting from is not Church growth, it is growth based on relocation of anxious, frightened and maybe prejudiced people.

Some of it is caused, without a doubt, by the overall effects of what I have described above, but some of it is located in the head and the heart and it is there that change must come. Paul Sweeney asked the question about Protestants leaving the city side of Derry: 'Were they pushed or did they jump?' It was probably a bit of both. We need to get off our tip-toes. If we are not so ready to jump we will not be so easily pushed. We need to learn the value of living together, of being enriched by each other, rather than being threatened by each other.

In some areas people have moved because of intimidation. Much of the movement of populations in Belfast has been due to intimidation. The peace walls of Belfast are not like the Berlin Wall: they were built because people wanted to feel safe. In some places Presbyterians, like many other people, were burned and intimidated out of their homes. But in some other areas it appears that Presbyterians do not wish to be outnumbered by their Catholic neighbours. Catholics often move into what were largely Protestant areas: they seem to be unconcerned about being outnumbered. When the percentage of Catholics increases in some middle-class urban areas,

Presbyterians, along with other Protestants, stop buying houses in those areas while others move out, leaving Presbyterian churches and controlled schools marooned like islands in a surrounding sea of Catholic people.

What will happen when Catholics start to buy houses in these new areas to which Presbyterians have moved? Will it result in another retreat? Where will it end?

In addition to this, perhaps as many as 50 per cent of Presbyterian young people, involved in third-level education, are studying outside Northern Ireland. Queen's University and the University of Ulster have student populations which representatively are probably the reverse of the wider 60/40 Protestant/Catholic split of the population. Most of those who go to study in Great Britain do not return. As well as its general effect on the Protestant population, this will eventually have a serious impact on Presbyterian Church leadership.

This siege mentality, rooted in defensive thinking, will be the death of us all.

It is often said that the Church is supposed to be different from the surrounding environment. It is supposed to be a counter culture, renewing the whole body politic. Instead of the Church influencing the culture, we have adopted the pervasive siege culture. Instead of asking 'How in the sovereign purposes of God are Presbyterian people to influence and contribute to the health of the whole Church and the whole community?' we appear to be retreating into separation, erroneously imagining that there is security and strength in isolation.

Instead of advocating withdrawal, the New Testament bears witness to the Church engaging with the wider society and crossing religious, political and cultural frontiers, not withdrawing behind them. Sustainable evangelism is not consistent with a defensive siege mentality.

We need to evolve an ideological construct or mental attitude which is rooted in reformed convictions about individual liberty and is capable of accommodating diversity. It may be like the

Presbyterian thinking which helped to shape notions of liberty and diversity in the early days of American independence. It will have relevance for the whole of Ireland, but perhaps have more impact on Northern Ireland where there are a higher percentage of Presbyterians.

This will require a change of mind and a fundamental revision of the prevailing ideological construct of siege, isolation and defensive thinking. Instead of desiring to live in homogeneous cultural and religious communities, we need to welcome inclusive societies which embrace diversity and, in turn, lead to enrichment as we seek peace, justice, security and honour for everyone.

There is no security for Presbyterians which does not embrace security for everyone; no justice for Presbyterians which does not include justice for everyone; no wellbeing for Presbyterians which does not include wellbeing for everyone.[14]

6

PEOPLE OF THE WORD

LET YOUR WORDS BE FEW

The Word of God is central in Presbyterian thinking. In most Presbyterian churches the pulpit is in a central and dominating place. The reading and preaching of the scriptures probably occupy between one third and one half of the service. Theology is tested against the Word of God and preaching is based upon the scriptures. Presbyterians need to beware of bibliolatry, remembering that the 'Word' became flesh in ways in which it never became a book. Where other religions have sacred places, Presbyterians have a sacred book, which can be found in any place and is frequently found in the home; unfortunately, less frequently read than used to be the case.

Presbyterians used to be reticient about calling a building a church. The building was the 'meeting house'; the church was the people of God. This shifts the location of what is holy from a place to the Bible and to people.

The name of God is held in reverence. A Presbyterian will be reluctant to use the name of God in a loose or familiar way. Seldom will you hear a Presbyterian say 'God bless'. God's name is not used as a method of saying farewell. Presbyterian religion is not worn on the sleeve, nor, dare one say it, even sometimes on the tongue. The ideal is that it should be lived in a quality of life marked by honesty and integrity.

Being careful with words, Presbyterians follow the preacher's injunction in Ecclesiastes 'Think before you speak and... don't say any more than you have to' (Ecclesiastes 5:2) and Christ's words: 'Let your communication be Yea, yea; Nay, nay'; for whatsoever is more than these cometh of evil' (Matthew 5:37).

This careful attention to words, their meanings and their implications leads to documents being written and read carefully. Presbyterians do not live easily with studied ambiguity. Long periods of time are taken up in the General Board (the most representative board after the General Assembly) struggling over words before they are issued to the press, even though it is likely that not much attention will be paid to them.

Presbyterians are suspicious of those who come bearing a wealth of vocabulary, wondering what might be hidden in the multiplicity of words. If it can't be said simply, perhaps there is something to hide.

To say that they are suspicious of words, is not to say that they are suspicious of learning or of science: perhaps the desire for precision is a precondition for accurate scientific enquiry. The Scottish Reformation nurtured the learning of the Scottish universities. The Presbyterian Church has always insisted that its ministers should be people with a university education, and possess a university degree in another academic discipline to place alongside divinity. In the early days the sons of farmers crossed the Irish Sea and travelled to Glasgow with a bag of meal for sustenance during the university term.

This culture has not produced many poets, authors or artists. It is a culture more interested in engineering than in art; more likely to rejoice in the launch of a ship than the production of a painting. Presbyterians have a tendency to tame whatever they touch, clipping hedges and draining fields. They don't like too much untidiness.

Presbyterian suspicion of art may go back to the post-Reformation suspicion of symbolism which tended to encourage the use of the imagination. When the imagination is let loose, the mind may no longer be controlled by the Word. After the Reformation, statues and images were ruthlessly removed from churches, because of the second commandment warning against the production of 'any graven image, or any likenesses of anything that is in heaven above, or that is in the earth beneath'.

Presbyterian worship is simple and dignified and their meeting houses normally simple in style and functional in furnishings, being almost devoid of ornamentation apart from stained-glass windows. Even though the Reformed faith emphasises both 'Word and Sacrament', and it is to the ministry of both that a minister is ordained, a baptismal font and a communion table will seldom be as visible as a pulpit.

It is only within the last hundred years that most Presbyterian congregations have added hymns and songs to the psalms in worship. Controversies raged in the General Assembly and in congregations before the decisions were taken to depart from the sole use of metrical psalms and to permit organs to accompany congregational praise. Most ministers wear black gowns and white Geneva bands denoting ordination. Ministers wear very similar robes, so no one is distracted from what is being said, by elegant suits, flashy ties or resplendent vestments. Sometimes the sombre black is relieved by the colour of an academic hood; but that's it.

The exception to the tendency to use as few words as possible may be found in the multiplicity of words used in worship in days gone by, when sermons could last for an hour or more, and extemporary prayers for twenty minutes. The pulpit was often the primary place where people were taught the contents and complexities of the faith. The sermon was not designed to entertain the congregation, which gathered with serious intent to apply themselves to what was being said.

Preaching is not one-way traffic from the pulpit to a passive pew: listening requires effort. Not only must old time preachers have been wordsmiths, the people must have been used to assimilating words. That aspect of Presbyterianism does not speak of a verbally impoverished people. The words of the preacher were listened to carefully and often discussed later.

A story is told about how Francis Hutcheson, who later became Professor of Moral Philosophy at the University of Glasgow, was sent as a young preacher by his father, the minister of Downpatrick and later Armagh, who was afflicted with rheumatism, as a substitute to conduct the service.

> The weather clearing meanwhile, the father, out of paternal curiosity, proceeded towards the church, two miles distant, that he might collect the opinions of his hearers as to the pulpit powers of his son. Mr Hutcheson was surprised to meet the people returning home long before the usual hour for dismissal. He interviewed an elder, a Scotsman, concerning this remarkable occurrence, and received as reply, 'Your silly son, Frank, has fashed a' the congregation with his idle cackle; for he has been babblin' this oor aboot a good and benevolent God and that the sauls o' the heathen themselves will gang tae heaven if they follow the licht o' their ain consciences. Not a word does the daft boy ken, speer, nor say about the gude auld comfortable doctrines of election, reprobation, original sin, and faith.'[1]

Should a worshipper be blind, very little would be missed in a Presbyterian worship service: it is dominated by words. It is easy to broadcast a Presbyterian service on the radio, but places great demands on a television producer, for practically nothing moves in the service, and there is very little of interest to see, apart from the faces of the congregation.

Nor are Presbyterians much given to statements of elaborate praise. They are suspicious of a culture which gives a greater priority to maintaining relationships than to being absolutely honest. This may well be a reason for the fractured nature of the Protestant part of northern Irish society, which is marked by the existence of many churches and mission halls and of many varieties of unionism. Catholic culture, on the other hand, is much more unified and cohesive, more capable of mobilisation, more given to corporate responses and more capable of accommodating diversity. It has consequently been more difficult to organise community development groups in Protestant than in Catholic areas of Belfast. Protestant society is deeply individualistic.

THE STRICT BEAT OF SCHOLASTIC THOROUGHNESS

This raises the question of the place of imagination in worship and theological reflection and the use of material in the service which stimulates reflective, imaginative, lateral thought, rather than providing existing answers to questions previously posed.

Some people seem to be of the opinion that anything worth thinking has already been thought and all that is required of us is to learn from the theologians and leaders of the past and reproduce the certainties which they have already determined. There is no doubt that this is popular and reassuring for some people. It is like the certainty provided by a Church which claims infallibility for some of its teachings.

Presbyterianism, on the other hand, holds all its theological statements to be subordinate to the scriptures. It does not take too much study of the scriptures to ascertain that they contain much reflective material as people have wrestled with God through sermons, praise and prayer, and with the implications of faith in an uncertain world. They contain the Gospels, the Epistles, apocalyptic imagery of Ezekiel and Revelation, the poetry of the Psalms, yearning and complaint, hope and celebration, forgiveness and accusation, prophesy and wisdom. It takes imagination to understand what it's about. Among other things, the Bible is the book of a pilgrim people. A church which takes the Bible as its primary source material cannot help but be on an adventure of faith . . . unless of course it has decided that the theologically 'sound' authority has already given the definitive answers to absolutely everything.

Justo Gonzalez, a Latin American evangelical theologian, in an introduction to a book of sermons from the 'perspective of liberation theology' explains the process of theological reformation which liberation theologians (including Third World evangelicals) have undergone, when they have reflected upon the teaching of scripture in situations far removed from the economic centres of power and of western theological traditions.

> Like most Christians they grew up in a church that took for granted that it already knew, at least in broad outline, what the Bible said. All one needed to do was read more of the Bible in order to fill in the outline and to gain inspiration. But the church did not expect to find anything radically new. However, as liberation theologians became aware of the insights that developed into liberation theology, they began discovering that the outline of biblical teaching which the church had given them was not exact, that there was a great deal in the Bible that the outline did not include and a great deal more that it misinterpreted . . . When these people began to understand the radical nature of the biblical word, every text, no matter how well known previously, spoke a new word. Indeed, once more, the Bible, which the church had grown used to handling as a familiar book, became the awesome Word of God, coming to our day from beyond our present social structures, judging both these structures and us.[2]

Seán Quinlan wrote in the *Furrow* about the big hoardings in cities which proclaim, between advertisments for automobiles and Scotch, that 'the wages of sin is death' (Romans 6.23). He wrote: 'They stare at you from the frozen isolation of print, lone rangers armed with menace.'[3] But the gospel is not so much armed with menace as filled with generosity. The point of the message in Romans, which continues: 'but the gift of God is eternal life', is the contrast between the stupendous generosity of God and the miserable wages which sin pays. Sin is not only 'any want of conformity unto, or transgression of, the law of God',[4] it is also the abuse of grace.

Christianity which is locked into interpretations of sin as transgression of law rather than as violation of grace produces a society described in these words by John Hewitt as he looked back on Belfast from Coventry:

> A full year since, I took this eager city,
> the tolerance that laced its blatant roar,
> its famous steeples and its web of girders,
> as image of the state hope argued for,
> and scarcely flung a bitter thought behind me
> on all that flaws the glory and the grace
> which ribbons through the sick, guilt-clotted legend
> of my creed-haunted, godforsaken race.[5]

The Presbyterian *Shorter Catechism* describes God without any mention of love. 'God is a Spirit, infinite, eternal and unchangeable, in His being, wisdom, power, holiness, justice, goodness and truth.'[6] The definition is all right as far as it goes, but it hardly goes far enough. People need to be persuaded that God's grace comes before any repentance, faith or obedience on their part: that is why grace can be depended upon.

The result of this kind of theology is that some people do not know where they stand with God. A goodly number of people who worship in Presbyterian churches are not communicant members of the church. Some people may attend worship but stay away from communion, feeling safer at a distance in case they shouldn't be there at all. They take the warnings given in 1 Corinthians 11:28–9 about eating and drinking without self-examination and thereby eating and drinking judgement on themselves as warnings against imperfection, rather than as warnings against dividing the body of Christ, the original context of the warnings. If there is no security in the grace of the gospel offered in the communion service, there is no security anywhere, and definitely not at home or at the back of the church.

On Good Friday, 5 April 1985, Oliver Messiaen was interviewed on *The South Bank Show* in a programme entitled 'Music of Faith'. He spoke of the radiance of Christ at the Transfiguration and the Resurrection being like the radiance of snow in bright sunlight, which is nothing compared with the radiance of the sun itself. He described a glorified body as one with 'agility'. In the prison camp where Messiaen was interned during the Second World War he composed a *Quartet for the End of Time*. They would not have had adequate instruments in the prison to perform the work – indeed he might have been killed before it could be performed – but he said, 'Even if I died, I knew there would be paradise . . . it is certain . . . joy exists beyond sorrow . . . beauty beyond horror.'

What an eloquent testimony of Christian hope. All preaching and Christian worship, all celebration of the sacraments should be marked with the agility of the Transfiguration and Resurrection, and should be filled with Christian hope. 'But,' said Messiaen, 'strict beat belongs to the military march, which is unreal.' He said that his music belonged to birdsong which he likened to 'the branches of a tree or the waves on the sea, all of which are uneven'.

Irish Presbyterians are more influenced by the strict beat of scholastic thoroughness, than with the agility born of grace. If preaching is preoccupied with orthodoxy and is formed 'in conformity to the Standards rather than as the truth most surely to be believed',[7] it may produce congregations which are submissive to orthodox conformity rather than to the living truth 'most surely to be believed'. Might this not produce a culture of rigid inflexibility rather than a community of faith ready for journeys?

This is not unrelated to our understanding of God. If we think primarily in terms of sovereignty, power and authority and overlook relational concepts which lie at the heart of the Trinity, we are not likely to produce congregations and communities which stress the importance of relationships. For example, the nature of the relationships between a child and a parent ought not to be primarily those of authority and submissiveness. Children ought to obey their parents and parents ought to provide a secure environment which will include boundaries, but the relationship ought to be marked by warmth and love which encourage obedience, love, trust, freedom and creativity.

God has given us the capacity to imagine as well as to think logically. The left and right hemispheres of the brain work in two different ways. In most people the left hemisphere functions logically and analytically and looks for literal meanings. The right hemisphere processes information holistically. Many scientific breakthroughs come from intuitive, artistic imagination located in the right hemisphere and not from logical deduction.

Theology which is dominated by the left hemisphere will be logical and rigid and its associated preaching will be analytical. Right-brain theology will be imaginative and creative. While the first kind will be deadly dull, there is no way the second can be checked against anything. What is needed is a dynamic relationship between both.

Presbyterianism is marked by too much left-brain strict beat. We could do with more of our life marked by agility; more affirmation of joy beyond sorrow; more celebration of apocalyptic extravagance using the doxologies sung by choirs composed of millions from all over the earth (Revelation 5:11–13). More of that emphasis on 'blessing, and honour, and glory, and power' might provide us with a mindset which could celebrate diversity and make space for legitimate difference.

The 'Mission Statement' received by the General Assembly at its meeting in 1992 to mark the 350th anniversary of the first presbytery in Ireland acknowledged God's call to his Church to worship Him

... with our whole lives, meeting together in groups large and small and gathering especially on the Lord's Day for the preaching and study of His word, the celebration of the sacraments and the offering of prayer and praise with reverence and joy, using language, form and music appropriate both to Scripture and to our time and culture.[8]

Protestantism which is characterised by an exclusive emphasis on 'Correct Doctrine' is described by the Brazilian theologian Rubem Alves as being conservative on two levels. 'On the one hand it evidences institutional and religious limitations – a resistance to any innovation, sacralizing thought forms which it has inherited from the past. At this level it also establishes institutional control mechanisms in order to eliminate every manifestation of deviant thought and conduct. On the other hand . . . [it] expresses itself in a legitimization of the dominant political powers, with a total absence of prophetic criticism.'[9]

Such an alliance of conservatism in Church and political life has been a characteristic of much ecclesiastical and political life in Ireland. It has been a significant source of resistance to necessary change in the last twenty years. When a society understands itself to be threatened, it may well revert to old convictions which represent an ideological mix of culture, politics and theology which may not represent what God requires in that new situation.

At an official state level this can take the form of 'state religion' which is facilitated by succumbing to what David Claerbout calls the 'privatisation myth'. Here the Church clings to a private individualistic notion of sin. The biblical dimension of solidarity and complicity in sin is theoretically recognised in the concept of original sin but is not contemporaneously applied. 'Our cultural heritage of individualism minimises the element of rebellion and antagonism to God to the private not to corporate, to the personal not the structural dimension of human life.'[10] A personally upright person can thus become an unthinking servant of a thoroughly corrupt state.

The Word of God can continue to break open all kinds of Church traditions in surprising ways as people find that the scriptures speak a very different language than what they had previously taken for granted. This process is greatly hindered by a defensive mindset which believes in the *de facto* infallibility of a Church's tradition and customs.

7

CULTURES OF HOSPITALITY
AND CONDITIONALITY

ALL OR ONLY SOME?

Issues of religion, identity, culture and behaviour are inter-woven. The Irish Catholic culture strikes an outsider like me as being very cohesive in a way the Presbyterian culture is not. There are two quite different senses of belonging in the two communities. There is a universal sense of belonging in the Catholic community, whereas the Protestant sense of belonging is much more conditional.

Catholics look upon all baptised people as regenerate Christians. After baptism, Catholics are required to live out the implications of their baptism and be what they already are. All baptised people are understood to belong to Christ and to the Church, and since almost everyone in the wider community has been baptised, the membership of the community and the Church is more or less the same.

The Presbyterian understanding shares some of this, but with some differences. Presbyterians believe that baptism is a sacrament of the New Testament; it admits the individual into the visible Church and is '. . . a sign and seal of the covenant of grace, of . . . ingrafting into Christ, of regeneration, of remission of sins'.[1] However, the Church cannot control grace, nor does baptism automatically guarantee salvation. The baptised Presbyterian knows that subsequent to baptism, he or she is required, by the power of the Holy Spirit, to embrace Jesus Christ as he is offered in the gospel. It is through the preaching of the gospel that the good news of the unconditional love of God is announced to the world. It is to each individual person that the call to repentance is addressed and the offer of salvation is made. This introduces into the equation the issue of that individual's response to Christ. It is not enough to say that we have been baptised, we must also exercise and profess our faith and only then is the circle completed.

This means that in any Presbyterian community there are two groups of people. First, there are baptised people who have exercised their faith in Christ and have publicly professed the same and been admitted by the local kirk session into the communicant membership of the Church. Second, since not every baptised person has made that profession of faith, there are those who, while in one sense being still a part of the family, do not, in fact, have a right to all the privileges or the responsibilities of the Church. Many may support the Church in all kinds of ways; some may even worship regularly and many do; but until faith is both exercised and publicly professed to the kirk session, and a commitment is made to the Church and to Christ, such people are semi-detached and some are in the far country.

Catholics are offended whenever some Presbyterians say that Catholics may not be Christians. That statement must be understood in the light of the fact that many Presbyterians say the same thing about themselves, meaning that they have not yet made a personal commitment to Christ. In a profoundly important way, the individual, raised within the community of faith, must make a personal response to God which touches the very core of that person's individuality. At that point lie the roots of Presbyterian individual accountability to God and acceptance by God. In that matter, Jesus Christ alone is the mediating priest, and the individual concerned enters into the privileges and responsibilities of the corporate priesthood of the Church. That calling to priesthood is shared with all who believe and is to be expressed in the whole of life: in the Church; in business; in the professions; in work of all kinds; in the home and in all of one's relationships with other people. It carries with it a deep sense of duty rather than a concern for rights.

While Presbyterian Church discipline is not now exercised with the rigour which obtained in the past, should an individual live in a way which causes a scandal to the gospel, the kirk session can suspend that person from attendance at communion, until such time as that person shows evidence of repentance. Nowadays people will more often absent themselves from church services.

I suspect that the Catholic culture of hospitality is gentler and more accommodating with sinners. In that culture of hospitality, everyone seems to belong: no one is put outside. Even IRA gunmen are part of the family, after all. If they are killed, the Church does not condone what they have done but neither does it disown them; it compassionately prays for them. The explanation given by the Catholic Church on this issue of the funerals of paramilitary members is welcome, for the practice is open to misinterpretation.

Presbyterian belonging is much more conditional. In Presbyterian culture many are outsiders. The Church and the society of which the Church is a part are not one and the same thing.

I know of one incident, where a loyalist paramilitary member was murdered. The man's family were committed members of the local Presbyterian church: he was not. The minister made it clear that if there were to be any paramilitary displays during any part of the funeral he would not take the service. The normal practice in that family of having the funeral from the home was to be followed. (It is a more recent, and by no means universal, practice to have funerals from Presbyterian churches.) The minister's pastoral visits to the home were frequent, and appreciated. Once the paramilitary organisation indicated that they intended to have a display of some kind during the funeral, the family said they did not expect their minister to be involved. They had no wish for the Church to be identified in any way with that kind of display. They did not want their Church compromised.

But then, you might ask, is the Church not the place where sinners find hospitality? Indeed. But on what terms?

There is something attractive about the culture of Catholic hospitality. It is much more relaxed and accepting than the 'up-tightness' of Presbyterian precision. It is marked by generosity and an ability to enjoy life. Of course things may not always be as they appear to be on the surface. Presbyterian precision may mask a hidden generosity of spirit. I am assured that the surface relaxed culture of Catholic Ireland may at times hide a deeper hidden unexpressed animosity towards neighbours or acquaint-ances. Beneath the romantic hospitality there can lurk the bit-terness of ancient memory and local resentments about boundaries and the ownership of fields.

LANGUAGE AND RELATIONSHIPS

The Protestant emphasis upon the importance of 'the Word' affects their use of language, which is sparing in its use of am-biguity. One is supposed to say as clearly as possible what is meant, with the consequences being understood, and one is to live by one's word.

W.R. Rodgers expressed the abrupt nature of the speech:

> I am Ulster, my people are an abrupt people
> Who like the spiky consonants in speech
> And think the soft ones cissy; who dig
> The *k* and *t* in orchestra, detect sin
> In sinfonia, get a kick out of
> Tin cans, fricatives, fornication, staccato talk.
> Anything that gives or takes attack,

> Like Micks, Tagues, tinker gets, Vatican.
> An angular people, brusque and Protestant,
> For whom the word is still a fighting word,
> Who bristle into reticence at the sound
> Of the round gift of the gab in Southern mouths . . .[2]

All language is conditioned by the culture within which it is shared. There are many ways of using language. For some people, language is a symbolic means of pointing to the truth, which is greater and more complex than the language used. Language is like a signpost which points away from itself. To see the truth you have to look where the language points. For some other people, the truth lies within the language, so instead of looking where the language points, you look deeper and deeper into the language, taking its meaning literally. I have most sympathy with the first way. I think that many Presbyterians live within the second.

For others, language is more complex still, providing space between the lines, leaving room for interpretation, not tying people down with many assumed presuppositions. Fundamentalist discourse is different again, being often most marked by the declamatory style of its delivery and its intolerance of perceived and identified enemies.

The Presbyterian Church is both a faith-based community and a belief-based community, and those beliefs are expressed in a set of words. The relationships within the Church are moderated by the linguistics as well as by God, that is, by the Bible, the Westminster Confession of Faith and the Code as well as by the Trinity.

The Basic Code of the Church (Section III:12) states:

> The Presbyterian Church in Ireland, as a witness for Christ, has adopted subordinate standards in which is set forth what she understands the Word of God to teach on certain important points of doctrine and worship. These subordinate standards serve as a testimony for truth and against error and serve as a bond of union for members of the Church.

It does not say that the subordinate standards are *the* bond of union, which is in Christ, but they are *a* bond of union, and one that is not unimportant.

There is a difference of emphasis when we compare the Presbyterian and Catholic communities on the issue of the priority given to Church allegiance as against theological statements. Many Catholics find it possible to stay within the Catholic Church while disagreeing with some of its teachings and some of the statements in papal encyclicals. Many Protestants would be much more likely to leave a denomination or a congregation if they disagreed with statements made or policies pursued. The Church divided at the Reformation over theological issues. The search for theological precision is obvious to anyone who has much contact with Presbyterianism.

Barry White, after an interview with Padraig O'Malley, the influential Irish-American expert on divided societies, reported O'Malley's conviction that ' "language is central to the lack of understanding between Roman Catholics and Protestants. Nationalist leaders talk about 'frameworks' while unionists prefer to deal with definite proposals. The two approaches can be traced back to their theological roots before and after the Reformation." . . . He argues that if the religious element is not addressed, it could seriously handicap the search for a solution . . . If any progress was to be made in talks, the two sides would have to understand each other, knowing that they used language in two different ways, coming from different modes of thought . . . "Both the Anglo-Irish Agreement and the Downing Street Declaration were written in a language which Protestants could not understand. They were devised to allow for latitude – and that's what Protestants can't deal with." '[3]

Presbyterians have difficulty with this way of proceeding. They are much less likely to separate form and substance. For them, the meaning of a document is the sum total of the words used. If they want to understand it, they don't ask what it is getting at, they don't look for spaces, they delve into the meaning of the words. This is not unimportant when it comes to evaluating political documents. Is it the case that the intention of a document may be as important as the words used; is it important to look for spaces as well as prescriptions? Those reading documents need to understand the people who wrote them otherwise they will not interpret them properly; similarly, if we are writing documents which we want to be understood, we must bear the readers in mind.

Presbyterians like the words to be precise. Generally, they try to get the language right first and then build the relationships. If they can't agree on the words, then the relationships suffer, even disintegrate. Others may have a different way of approaching this. For them, relationships come first and words are then found which meet the perceived needs of the hour to keep the relationships intact.

There are times when one needs to be precise and accurate, but the demand for too much precision at all times may result in deadlock. Compromise becomes impossible. There are other times when creative flexibility is needed to give people necessary space; but too much of it may cover duplicity and lead ultimately to the total destruction of trust. It takes great wisdom to interpret the signals within the words.

LANGUAGE AND TRUST

There are very deep layers of mistrust in our society. They exist across the divisions within Northern Ireland and between the north and the south. They also exist between Ireland and England. The possibility that Albion is being perfidious can't be far from the minds of the officials in the Department of Foreign Affairs in Dublin.

Nor are unionists likely to have unlimited trust in the reassurances of British ministers. On the 16 November 1993 the Northern Ireland Secretary said: '... there has been no negotiaton with Sinn Féin. No official ... has been talking to Sinn Féin on behalf of the British Government . . .' This denial was repeated on 22 November 1993. The denial proved to be untrue. When the details of the discussions were subsequently published by both sides, even then the two accounts did not correspond.

In analysing the political processes in the Republic of Ireland which led to the collapse of the coalition government at the end of 1994, the *Irish Times* journalist John Waters explored the difficulty that the political process gets into when politicians behave as if substance does not matter. He wrote that in political discourse it appears sometimes that: 'As in poker, it is not always necessary to have substance on your side, so long as the illusion of substance can be maintained in language.' The trouble is that the public may not recognise this, and the result, in Waters's words, is a 'serious disjunction between words and meaning in politics'.[4]

Presbyterian language does not have too many layers to it; it does not possess too much flexibility. Presbyterians may not be very good negotiators. Their opening statements tend to contain an analysis of the situation along with the bottom line. There is no movement either contemplated or even possible, unless you can convince them that the analysis is wrong. If you can't convince them of that, the bottom line will not move, on principle.

There is both strength and weakness in this. The strength is that everyone knows where everyone stands. The weakness is that people from this tradition may be inflexible, even when flexibility and compromise are to everyone's advantage.

Jesus said on one occasion, 'If someone brings a lawsuit against you and takes you to court, settle the dispute with him while there is time, before you get to the court' (Matthew 5:25). This suggests two things to me. Firstly, that one's self-interest is often served by settling matters, and secondly, that failure to grasp the opportunity to settle may lead to even greater problems. Self-interested intelligent flexibility is required. There are times when intransigence is a sign of weakness and not of strength . . . There are times when a refusal to try to settle with an opponent is not in the interests of either party.

One of the suspicions held by Presbyterians is that too much flexibility causes problems and destroys trust. Nuala O'Faolain wrote about these suspicions:

> ... you do, of course, hear criticism of Catholicism in Northern Ireland ... partly it is the conviction that Irish Catholics have an ambiguous relationship with facts – with the truth ...
>
> I'd say I'm typical of southerners in hardly ever thinking of Catholicism as a determinate. Catholicism just is. It sits there. Beside it sits the political and legal and economic and cultural thing which we call our society. It never crosses anyone's mind to comment that most of the people involved in business scandals, say, or planning scandals, or tax evasion scandals, are practising Roman Catholics. What has that got to do with anything, people would say? ... Nothing. The one has nothing to do with the other.[5]

People in all societies look out on the world through the tinted spectacles of culture, which includes religion. Since we wear these cultural spectacles from birth we are unaware of the cultural tints. It is often only when we go to another society which has differently tinted spectacles that we become aware of our own.

My experience in Jamaica, a post-colonial society where I worked for ten years as a minister, taught me to be aware of the complex layers of creativity in the ordinary discourse of a culture different from my own. I shared these reflections with a BBC Radio 4 audience one morning on *Thought for the Day* at a time when people were trying to decide whether the IRA ceasefire was 'total' or 'permanent' and the Taoiseach, Albert Reynolds, had declared that it was 'all over'.

One afternoon in the village where we lived I met a man who had not attended church for a long time. 'Minister,' he said, 'I'll be at church on Sunday.' I had heard this on a number of occasions before and I knew that he had no intention of coming; not only that, he knew that I knew he wasn't coming, and I also knew that he knew that I knew.

What was I to do? I might have pinned him verbally to the wall and sought reassurances about his intentions. But that would have been both unhelpful and culturally inappropriate. He was, after all, giving me my place as his minister. I, in turn, was required to give him space to decide whether or not he would come.

To say that he was telling me lies would be to misunderstand the subtle nature of the relationship and the dialogue. There were dangers in the subtlety, for if the man engaged in that kind of discourse all the time, no one, including himself, would know at any time when to take him seriously.[6]

There is an associated issue about the law. Terence McCaughey locates the origin of the problem in Ireland, not in the Church or in theology, but in the experience of a colonised population.

> People who, under the British administration, had sat easily to the State and its laws, continued to do so after independence – giving rise to the Irish antinomianism which foreign visitors have found so entertaining and quaint. Obedience to the Church was, on the whole, given more readily, and it is only recently that even a significant minority have sat as easily to the regulations and practices of the Church as they have always done to those of the State.[7]

A southern business executive, of Protestant extraction, but not now a member of any Church, put it to me this way:

> Our ambivalence to the law also derives from centuries of occupation, where the laws of the land were not 'owned' but imposed by a foreign force representing a foreign culture. People learnt to pay lip service to the law but then to behave completely differently. The ambivalence is deep-rooted in our culture.

I think that, on the whole, Presbyterians share with many other people the belief that laws are not there to express an ideal which one may or may not aspire to keep or find a way around; laws are meant to be kept. It might also be argued that people who are on the defensive, needing to know where they are, require precision in these matters.

If the building of confidence is a necesary precondition for political accommodation, the consolidation of trust is a necessary part of that. In that matter words are important. If people cannot trust what is being said, what then? But then maybe the problem lies in the interpretation. Maybe so. But maybe not.

8

IDENTITY: BELONGING
AND EXCLUSION

Identity is about self-understanding; about an individual's sense of place and of belonging. Since to be human is to be in relationships with other people, identity has a community dimension to it.

If a community is to be at peace, the issue of identity has to be handled sensitively. The people of these islands, and especially the people in Ireland, are in conflict because these issues have neither been handled well nor satisfactorily re-solved. Many people in Ireland feel excluded, believing that the universals of being Irish or British either do not or would not accommodate their particular identities.

Identity carries within it the memory of the community of which the individual is a part. Ray Davey of the Corrymeela Community calls it an issue of 'mythic consciousness'. In Ireland it has been associated with nationalist and unionist, loyalist and republican ideologies which have been the driving forces behind political commitment. It finds expression in both constitutional politics and violence. It is highly emotive, for it is often associated with flags and emblems and anthems, with space and territory.

The socialisation process is universal. When a child is born he or she goes through a socialisation process in which personal, family and community identities are shaped. The child learns to identify the self which belongs with this family and not that one; with this house and not that one; with this Church and not that one; with this school and not that one; with this community and not that one.[1]

There is no reason why this process should, in principle, be marked by conflict, provided these families, Churches, schools and communities are living in harmony with one another. The socialisation process can be enriching when each particularity finds space alongside and in harmony with others.

In Ireland this has not always happened. At almost all of these levels – family, Church, school, community – there has been volatility and the potential for conflict. Occasionally the volatility of the components has been carefully handled, the diversity has been recognised, identified, owned and creatively accommodated. At other times there has developed the culture of politeness which has avoided any mention of the problems outside a safe circle of trusted friends. The consequence of this is that prejudice or political ideology has been incestuously nurtured, accepted opinions not challenged, and misunderstandings, bigotries and stereotypings reinforced.

The Irish Inter-church Meeting's discussion document on sectarianism explains how sectarian attitudes can be learned within the home, through the casual remark dropped here or there in response to a face on television or a voice on the radio. Thus does a child learn that those people over there are not only different, they are to be distrusted, even feared and hated, while those other people over there belong to us. Thus can otherwise decent people become people of prejudice.

When a society is marked by either violence or injustice the sense of solidarity with one group rather than another intensifies. If my brother or my mother was killed by one of 'them', it is likely that the communal distrust will intensify. I and my family and my community will rally round to provide support and sustenance. At that point it is important for one of 'them' to cross the line of rupture and distance themselves from what has been done and establish some sense of solidarity with my community. If that does not happen, then I might be forgiven for thinking that 'they' all agree with what has been done. Silence is interpreted as support. Should one of 'our sort' kill one of 'them' then I, in turn, need to go and do the equivalent, crossing the line.

This can be difficult, for maybe I am not normally in the business of crossing that line. If I have to attend the funeral, maybe I should go into 'their' church. That is not easy when the leadership of the Churches frowned upon this practice until recently. Nevertheless it has to be done.

SUB-IDENTITIES

In Ireland it is possible to speak of two communities. But there are many sub-communities within these larger groupings and the identification of these is important.

Marianne Elliott and Terence Brown in Field Day Pamphlets numbers 7 and 8 (Field Day Theatre Company, Derry, 1985) have argued for the recognition of the fact that Protestantism is not a monolith and that there is within it a distinctive Presbyterian identity. But within the larger Protestant religious identity, there is not only a Presbyterian identity, there are multitudes of churches and mission halls, each with a separate identity. Often they define themselves in terms of their areas of disagreement with others. The only reason for their separate existence may be because they disagree about something. This results in an emphasis upon difference.

A sect might be distinguished from a Church in this way: a sect is primarily dependent for its existence upon its sense of difference from another body, and draws its psychic energy from the constant reinforcement of the idea of difference. A Church, on the other hand, while aware of difference, is primarily driven and controlled by what it positively believes. Size has nothing to do with this. It is possible to live with a sectarian mindset within a large Church.

POSITIVE AND NEGATIVE ELEMENTS IN IDENTITY

Early experience is processed through the interpretive models provided by the community's socialisation processes. No one starts from scratch in making sense of the world. There are inevitably positive and negative elements in this process of identity formation: who I am and who I am not.

There is nothing unusual in identity having a negative element to it, for it is evidence that we are not the same as the people next door or the community on the other side of the mountains. We can quite correctly and indeed inevitably say who we are and who we are not. The problem arises when the negatives become dominant and are asked to carry too heavy a load of significance. We then become dependent upon the 'others' for a definition of 'ourselves'. When the 'others' are the people who have killed us, robbed us, humiliated us and threatened us, and the stories of all of those events are carried within the discourse and songs of our community, we load ourselves with the burdens of history and invest enormous amounts of emotional energy in the identity of our group.

Communal identities in Ireland have developed in opposition to each other. The socialisation processes have been conflictual. The frameworks within which we have worked up to now have been negatively defined and defensively determined. If we are to determine new relationships they will have to accommodate and not threaten diversity, otherwise they will be resisted. If people believe that any new proposed arrangements do not honour, protect and take the substance of their particularity seriously, those arrangements will be resisted.

In Catholic and Protestant communities, the positive and negative elements work in different and important ways.

People of a Catholic/nationalist identity are positively Irish, and Catholic, and, since Vatican II, not hostile to Protestant Churches or their ministers, unless a daughter or son wishes to marry one of them and then the liberalism and benevolence may be severely tested. The negative part is anti-British. Whatever else Irish Catholics may be, they are not British.

On the other hand, people of a Protestant/unionist identity are positively British and Protestant and to some degree Irish. They probably define themselves as being from Northern Ireland. The negative part is most strongly expressed in being not Catholic. Again, this is seen very clearly at a time of mixed marriage. Whatever else Protestant/unionists may be, they are not Catholic.

Provided the negatives do not outweigh the positives we may turn out to be self-confident people with a secure sense of our own identities and a respect for the identities of other people who are different from us. When the negatives seriously outweigh the positives, we then become dependent upon the perceived 'other' as a marker in our self-definition.

The result of this is that Catholic/nationalists have no great problem with ecumenism but they have difficulty coping with what is British. On the other side, Protestant/unionists have difficulty coping with ecumenism, for it requires them to overcome long-held negative attitudes about Catholicism.

The Irish have historically been as anti-British as Protestants have been anti-Catholic. This was the point made by Cardinal Ó Fiaich when he said that most of the religious bigotry was on the Protestant side while most of the political bigotry was on the Catholic side. When only the first half of the statement was reported it made startling headlines but constituted irresponsible journalism. When both parts of his statement are taken into account it indicates that all of us carry a fair weight of negative baggage.

It is through the community that generational memories are carried. Many Presbyterians, especially those over forty, like singing the metrical versions of the psalms, for they provide a strong sense of connectedness with their childhood and, through that, with their parents beside whom they stood when they first learned to sing the psalms; and behind them again with previous generations in Ireland and in Scotland. This sense of connectedness with the metrical psalms is so strong that you would be forgiven for thinking that King David had lived in Edinburgh and not in Jerusalem and that he was a Presbyterian and not a Jew.

Seamus Heaney in a lecture to the Ireland Funds' Conference in Cork in June 1989 spoke about

> the doubleness of our focus in Ireland, our capacity to live in two places at the one time and in two times at the one place . . .
>
> The Republic may indeed be a country of conference hotels, computer printouts, fax and fish kills, property deals and stereophonic discos; but it is also, to a greater or lesser extent, the locus of an imagined Ireland, a mythologically grounded and emotionally contoured island that belongs in art time, in story time, in the continuous present of a common, unthinking memory-life.[2]

This double focus can work constructively: the 'mythologically grounded and emotionally contoured island' can energise projects like the Ireland Funds. May it not also be the case that the same romantic mythological Ireland can give rise to the destructive action of Armalites, tilt switches and Semtex? To the northern Protestant mind the romantic mythological Ireland of dreams can manifest itself as nightmares of burnings-out and shootings; of neighbours who maybe cannot be trusted.

THE RELIGIOUS ELEMENT

The religious content of identity has been a crucial factor in conflict in this country for it carries some of the weight of identity.

David Stevens, the General Secretary of the Irish Council of Churches maintains that:

The religious assemblies of the Irish, Scots and English carry the memories of community experience, North and South. They are entwined with, cannot be separated from, the cultural and political histories of the different communities in Ireland. They have shaped everyone in this society, both believers and non-believers . . .

Religion is that which binds together. It has also brought diversity and divison in Ireland.[3]

Historically, the animosity of the Presbyterian Church to the Anglican Church was considerable. But the Protestant/Catholic divide is the more significant one.

Presbyterian theology and Church life have, to a significant degree, been a reaction to Catholicism. There has been considerable stress on the differences, which is one reason why many Presbyterians are suspicious of ecumenical contact with Rome, unless it can be established that change has occurred within the Roman Church.

The Westminster Confession of Faith, a linguistic expression of a belief system, was formulated in the light of the issues which raged at the time when it was written in the 1640s, when the Reformation and Counter-Reformation struggles were being carried on in the nation states of Europe. Its statements are formulated both to explain the Reformed faith and, at times, to differentiate it from Catholicism. There is no doubt that the statements of the Confession describing the Pope as Antichrist have influenced how Presbyterians have seen the Catholic Church.

In 1855 the General Assembly was asked to pronounce an opinion on whether or not the Catholic Church would be 'regarded by this Church as a constituent portion of the visible Kingdom of Christ, and the ordinances which her priesthood administered as valid ordinances'. In 1861 the Assembly decided 'almost unanimously' that the Church of Rome was indeed a Church of Christ. However, it continued to hold that the Catholic Church was in error on a number of points of doctrine.

In 1988 the General Assembly addressed the issue and in exercising the Church's right to interpret and explain her standards passed a resolution which

> . . . steadfastly proclaims the Lord Jesus Christ as the only King and Head of the Church. From this it follows that no mere man can be head thereof, and that any claim to such headship is unbiblical. The General Assembly, under God, reaffirm this teaching but declare further their understanding that the historical interpretation of the Pope of Rome as the personal and literal fulfilment of the biblical figure of 'the Anti-Christ' and 'the Man of Sin' is not manifestly evident from scripture. A variety of views has long been held on this topic consistent with a loyal regard for the authority of Holy Scripture and a genuine acceptance of Reformation standards.[4]

The intensity of emotion residing in some Protestant anti-Catholicism is frightening. It goes deeper than rationality and cannot be separated from the political issues and the associated violence in this country.

Presbyterianism has not been universally marked by that intensity of opposition. In 1863 the magazine of what has become the *Irish Mission* of the Presbyterian Church counted itself 'among those who hold that salvation is often found among the communion of the Church of Rome'. The magazine went on to emphasise its belief that that Church had members that were not only Christians but 'Christians of the most eminent attainments, the lustre of whose simple piety and self-denying zeal have shed a bright lustre on the very name of Christianity.'[5] The burden of the magazine's complaint against the Catholic Church was that it had superimposed upon the old majestic doctrines of the Christian faith what the magazine called the 'self-righteous doctrines and commandments of men'.

Much of the hostility between the Churches was mutual.

Catholic attitudes to Protestant Churches have, until comparatively recently, shown little generosity, and vice versa. It is not long ago that Catholics and Protestants would not enter one another's churches, even for the funeral services of their neighbours. In 1949 the funeral service of the Protestant former President of Ireland, Douglas Hyde, was marked by the members of the Irish government sitting outside St Patrick's Cathedral in their cars on the advice of the bishops. This would be unthinkable today.

Austin Clarke expressed it like this:

> . . . At the last bench
> Two Catholics, the French
> Ambassador and I, knelt down.
> The vergers waited. Outside.
> The hush of Dublin town,
> Professors of cap and gown,
> Costello, his Cabinet,
> In Government cars, hiding
> Around the corner, ready
> Tall hat in hand, dreading
> *Our Father* in English. Better
> Not hear that 'which' for 'who'
> And risk eternal doom.[6]

The Orange Order still binds its members to promise not to attend a worship service conducted by a priest which involves the celebration of the Mass. This prevents Orangemen attending the funeral or marriage services of their Catholic friends and neighbours. Members are also bound by a promise not to marry a Catholic. While most people now attend the funerals and weddings of their friends in churches other than their own, there remains a pronounced reluctance among many Presbyterian ministers to participate in leadership roles in ecumenical services of worship with Catholic priests, even when the services are not sacramental.

9

IDENTITY AND LOYALTY

This leads me on to the question of whether or not the macro-identities of Irishness and Britishness have been capable of accommodating important micro-identities represented by the religious and ethnic diversity of the people who live here. The discussion is about people and not about territory.

The belief that one should have a secure sense of one's own identity and self-worth is important. There are few things as disabling as to internalise and believe other people's negative evaluations of one's own significance and worth. Protest against and resistance to denigration and insult are significant contributions to the mental and spiritual wellbeing of people; whether individual children in a school or collective groups of people in society.

For nationalists and unionists these issues of identity and loyalty have to do with people's sense of belonging or not belonging; of feeling at home or feeling an outsider; of being included or excluded. Catholic nationalists see the island as their homeland. Those who are here have been here so long that they have no tribal memory of having been anywhere else, although the names and the history betray a mixture of origins.

Simon Lee, imagining himself inside unionist skin, suggested:

> Unionists see an archipelago, a constellation of islands off the
> mainland of Continental Europe . . . Unionists share with others
> in these islands a sense of place, of locality, of affection for where
> they were born and raised, for where they and their families and
> friends have built a life.[1]

British identity has a diversity within it which the English do
not always recognise. Some English people understand being
British and being English as one and the same thing. This attitude is demonstrated when the English rugby team enthusiast-
ically sing the British national anthem at Twickenham as if the
anthem belonged, in some exclusive sense, to the English.

It is well documented that many Irish people, excluded from
the territory of the Republic of Ireland but living in Northern
Ireland, do not feel at home in a British Northern Ireland and
wish to have their Irishness honoured. This may be because
their Irishness is not acknowledged, because they have been
discriminated against on grounds of their religion or it may be
that they are hostile to anything British on the island of Ireland.

David Stevens asked if the pain of change for Protestant
Churches in the Republic of Ireland had led to the suppression
of memory. What has happened to the family memories of
many Catholic people living in Northern Ireland whose family
members have served with distinction in the British Army or the
RUC? Am I right that such people are reluctant to declare these
associations in public?

Northern nationalists have difficulty identifying with the
British national anthem which contains the words:

> Send her victorious
> Happy and glorious
> Long to reign over us . . .

If unionists wish Irish nationalists to be incorporated within
an exclusively British environment in Northern Ireland, the
nationalists may reasonably protest such failure to accommodate their particular identity.

On the other hand, if nationalists have difficulty standing for or singing 'God Save the Queen' in Belfast, many unionists have the same problem standing for 'The Soldier's Song' at rugby internationals at Lansdowne Road in Dublin. They stand respectfully for the anthem of 'another' country, but in no way can it be said to represent the identity of all of the Irish rugby team on the field, or of all of the supporters of that team in the stands. References to 'cannon's roar and rifle's peal' are not hospitable concepts to people whose businesses have been blown to pieces and whose relatives have been killed in the name of Ireland.

Would it be easy to abandon it or substitute something more suitable? Maybe the Irish Rugby Football Union would run into the same problems as the Senate of Queen's University Belfast when the decision was taken in 1994, in the interest of inclusiveness, to substitute 'God Save the Queen' with the European anthem 'Ode to Joy'.

When the Irish hockey team plays internationals overseas they use 'Danny Boy' with which all the team can identify, unless international rules, like those governing the Olympic Games, require them to do otherwise, in which case, like it or not, they use 'The Soldier's Song'.

What are anthems about? Are they supposed to unite people? In divided societies with coherent minorities, they often fail to do so. Ideological requirements, as expressed in anthems, often fail to accommodate diversity.

UNIONISTS AND IRISHNESS

The presence of British unionists living on the island of Ireland, who constitute the majority of people living in Northern Ireland, and who do not consent to be incorporated into a united Ireland, presents enormous difficulties for the Irish, south and north. While unionists have a strong sense of being British, many do not wish to totally abandon the claim to some degree of Irish identity. They are, nevertheless, very ambivalent about the extent of their Irishness. Twenty-five years of IRA violence have, for many, all but destroyed whatever identification with Irishness there may have been.

Constitutional Irish nationalists have, over the last number of years, sought to come to terms with the existence of their unionist neighbours; this shift was reflected in the wording of the Downing Street Declaration, that a united Ireland can only come about with the consent of a majority of the people living in Northern Ireland.

How accommodating is Irish identity of diversity? It is possible to be Scottish and Welsh (and English) and British. Is it possible to be Irish and British at one and the same time?

Professor Terence Brown of Trinity College Dublin wrote:

> the nationalist mind-set customarily finds the idea of an Irish person readily identifying himself or herself as British an evident absurdity. For the nationalist is marching to a different drum, to a tune that owes much to the idea of England as colonial oppressor and almost nothing to the idea of Britain as a complex and changing state.

He wrote in the same article that unionists did not give up a strong sense of being both Irish and British in the early days after Partition, until Irish identity took on an exclusive dimension. At the same time unionist identity moved in the equivalent but opposite direction, eliminating the Irish element in its identity. He warns about confusing

> the unionist sense of identity with the unionist sense of loyalty. The unionist is loyal to the British crown as the symbolic expression of the constitutional reality of the British state in whose commonwealth the citizen and subject feels his or her interests are most likely to be protected. His or her identity is a different matter. And a rather confused matter it is . . . They resent accordingly, or did in the fairly recent past, the hi-jacking of what they believe a perfectly tenable idea – the idea of Irishness, broadly

defined, within the former United Kingdom of Great Britain and Ireland, and within the more recent United Kingdom of Great Britain and Northern Ireland – by a narrow, largely Catholic and aggressively Gaelic version of Irish identity.[2]

Terence Brown refers to the unionist sense of identity as being confused. Some unionists would maintain that it is complex, but not necessarily confused. They maintain that it is both British and Irish and is no more confusing than being both Irish and American. There is no reason why both cannot be held together, unless, of course, Irish nationalist ideology requires the elimination of this 'evident absurdity'.

This shift in identity is important. It affects how Presbyterians in Ireland understand themselves. The Presbyterian Church, like the other larger Churches, lives its life in two political jurisdictions and has attempted, with some success and some failure, to be a Church of the whole island, relating to two cultures. An old logo of the Presbyterian Church had a burning bush alongside an Irish harp and an Irish wolfhound. Over the years, the harp and the wolfhound have disappeared.

That part of the Presbyterian Church which is in the Republic of Ireland does not understand itself to be an outpost of the Church in Northern Ireland. The Church lives in two jurisdictions and its membership is composed of citizens of two countries.

Shifts in identity indicate that issues of belonging are not set in concrete. This is evident in the final chapter of Fionnuala O Connor's *In Search of a State: Catholics in Northern Ireland* where it seems that Catholic identity in Northern Ireland is in a state of flux.

Since Independence, almost all the people living in the Republic of Ireland have come to see themselves as Irish but not British. They have chosen to separate themselves from the British and have settled into a comfortable, confident, exclusive and excluding Irish identity. If all the people who live on this island are to have ownership of being Irish then the Irish people need to be redefined to include all the diverse people (including the British) who live on the island. This will mean escaping from the pervasive excluding ideology of Irish Catholic nationalism. Such modification of national identity will not be easy.

Redefinition of what it is to be Irish, is not without another difficulty. Unionists, who would, presumably, have to be included in a definition of Irishness, are far from sure that they wish to be included.

THE CHURCH AND IDEOLOGICAL CAPTIVITY

It is understandable,[3] given the relationship between nation states and either Catholicism or varieties of the Churches of the Reformation, that ideologies such as Catholic nationalism and Protestant unionism should have occurred in Ireland. While the pastor and the historian may say with honesty that such identification is understandable, we may equally say that it has been by no means helpful to the cause of the gospel and that we have to find some way out of the trap.

European nationalistic ideologies have proved more powerful than class or Church in their abilities to recruit people to their service. Once the nation state declares war, the local Churches usually stand up and salute, or pray for victory. It is a short step to the misuse of the notion of what is sacred, as people speak about sacred language, sacred boundaries, sacred blood and sacred destiny. God then becomes a national icon and ceases to be God.

In a series of lectures on 'Jeremiah', given at Princeton Theological Seminary in 1989, Walter Brueggemann of Columbia Theological Seminary in Decatur, Georgia, spoke of 'imagined contrivances' which he said were a combination of religion, economics, politics, culture, et cetera. It is by the use of such 'imagined contrivances', or 'ideological constructs', that we make some kind of sense out of the world and particularly

out of our part of the world. Nationalistic ideologies are ideological constructs and imagined contrivances.

Imagined contrivances are not themselves reality, but are,
said Brueggemann, so 'relentlessly and persistently imagined
that we come to think of them as reality'. They are expressed
in national anthems, associated with flags, sometimes identified with Churches and religion, and celebrated in story and
song. This is so basic to our understanding of reality that
Breuggemann described this as 'pre-reason and elemental. We
cling tenaciously to it', and we often benefit from it in a variety
of different ways. We look at the world through the spectacles
of such imagined contrivances and we so confuse them with
reality that we think that we see the world straight, as God sees
it, but we are often wrong.

Brueggemann suggested that the task of the preacher is
to follow the material in the scriptures, the stories and the
prophets, the Psalms, the gospels, et cetera, which give us alternative contrivances, alternative proposals of reality. As alternative contrivances were proposed in the past, and we have the
record of them in the Bible, they were often heard as 'subversive
and threatening', as when Moses suggested to the Egyptian
Pharoah that he ought to let the people of Israel go. Those who
carried the message later, like Jeremiah and Jesus, were
arrested, threatened or silenced.[4]

Given the way that the prevailing religious/ideological identities have been forged in Ireland, the challenge facing us is
whether or not we are capable of forging some new set of relationships which are not determined by what has gone before. It
will be difficult if we insist on using only the loyalist/unionist or
republican/nationalist spectacles which have been bequeathed
to us. Things are changing in Ireland and the Churches are a
part of the process of change.

Theology involves reflective thought about the present in the
light of the Word of God and the contemporary situation. The
ecclesiological relationships in Ireland are changing and very

significant changes are taking place in the thinking and behaviour of the people of Ireland and the United Kingdom. The
danger for the Churches is that we live in the past of poisoned
memory and settle down at ease in the Zions of two old-
fashioned contending ideological constructs which have resulted in and been consolidated by significant levels of conflict.

Instead of desiring to live in homogeneous cultural and
religious communities, we need to welcome inclusive societies
which embrace diversity and lead to enrichment as we seek
peace, justice, security and honour for everyone.

It bears repeating: there is no justice for Presbyterians which
does not include justice for everyone; no wellbeing for Presbyterians which does not include wellbeing for everyone. These
are rights which should be accorded to people because they are
made in the image of God, not because they belong to some
particular tribe or Church.

The challenge for us in this generation is whether or not we
can escape from exclusive and excluding ideologies, which
release base passions of the most prejudiced and violent kind,
into wider horizons which can recognise, defend, affirm and
celebrate diversity.

The Church's life is rooted in Jesus Christ who has been given
to the Church as Lord over all. It witnesses to a kingdom which
crosses frontiers of time, geography, culture and political
loyalties and yet must live its life in relationship to all of these
realities. Its primary purpose is to witness to Christ and
the Kingdom of God and to the values associated with that
Kingdom. Its vitality flows from the love of the Father, the grace
of the Son and the fellowship of the Holy Spirit.

10

THE SCARS OF THE TROUBLES

During the Church year 1992–93 I had the opportunity to travel widely within Ireland, visiting some of the congregations of the Presbyterian Church. I am left with two dominant memories.

The first is of a Church whose life is marked by commitment and, after the divisive traumas of the debates which convulsed the Church in the late 1970s and early 1980s about our membership of the World Council of Churches, considerable internal cohesion and vitality. This has been helped by the reflective, celebratory and relational characteristics of the special 150th anniversary Assembly held in Coleraine in September 1990.

The second is of a Church which has suffered from very significant shifts of population directly related to the violence of the IRA, although some shifts of Protestant population were a consequence of loyalist violence forcing Catholics to find new homes.

Not only was it my responsibility that year to conduct the funerals of some of the people murdered by the IRA, I was also conscious of the deep wells of grief within families and congregations which had seen the people they love prematurely laid to rest, often in the quiet churchyards beside the buildings where they worship Sunday by Sunday. People have often felt isolated and vulnerable.

One morning in the heart of the Troubles, Fr John McCullagh asked in a broadcast on BBC Radio Ulster's *Thought for the Day*:

> Isn't there something pathetically pitiful when any man decides to interrupt the eternal plan of God and end a human life completely out of season?

In some churches there are simple memorials to those who have been murdered by the IRA, young lives ended 'completely out of season'.

There are few things as heartbreaking as to see a father carry the coffin of his son from the church to the adjacent cemetery; or to see a mother sit in church with her arm round the shoulder of her daughter, no more than a child, while she herself stares with empty eyes into the middle distance, devastated by the death of her husband.

Presbyterians are not the only people to have been murdered. It is true of all the Churches. Many people whose lives have been ended in this way have been Catholics. Loyalist paramilitary violence has often been directed indiscriminately at members of the Catholic community. Since this book is written from within a Presbyterian perspective, I have tried to describe what it has been like to be on the receiving end of efficient republican violence. I know there are other stories.

The leadership of the IRA took a cleverly calculated, opportunistic decision to restart republican violence in 1971. The injustices and unrest at the time provided the opportunity but the conditions at the time could not be construed as justifying what was unleashed on the community. It is my belief that the opportunity was taken then, not so much to correct injustice and defend Catholic areas, as to attempt the completion of what the republican movement saw as the unfinished business of the early decades of the century: get the British out and unite the island. In pursuit of this goal republicans killed over nineteen hundred people, a significant number of them their fellow Catholics.

It is my conviction that republican violence was based upon a fundamentally flawed analysis of the challenges facing our society. The principal resistance to the realisation of the republican and nationalist dream of a united Ireland lies within Northern Ireland, and not in Britain. While there are a few Protestants who would like to see a united Ireland, the resistance to its realisation lies largely within the Protestant community. While republicans have said that their armed struggle is against the British, they have mostly killed their Protestant neighbours, destroyed their businesses and bombed their towns.

One of the most heartrending aspects of this campaign is the careful way in which individual people have been targeted. There is something chilling about a terrorist campaign which causes people efficiently to target victims who are often known to them, and then to decide the time and place of their deaths.

Republicans declare that they were not killing people because they were Protestants, but because they were in the police or in some branch of the security forces. The stark fact remains that most of them *were* Protestants. They were shot off tractors, in their cars, outside churches, in their businesses and in their homes. The more isolated the location, the easier the target. As far as most Presbyterians are concerned, republican reasoning about this simply exacerbates the sense of anger; and that for two reasons.

Firstly, to serve one's society in the security forces is seen as an honourable occupation, particularly so since there is a high degree of risk involved from day one. The wearing of a uniform destroys anonymity: the person is at risk twenty-four hours every day. The people who have served in this way are and have been part of the informal networking of any community.

Secondly, many of these people, as well as serving in the security forces, are not only the sons and daughters, brothers and sisters, fathers and mothers of other people, they are also members of congregations and sometimes leaders within the congregations. Paramilitaries don't just kill their so-called legitimate targets, they kill Sunday School teachers, youth leaders, church organists and members of kirk sessions.

Sometimes it seemed that prominent people were specifically targeted to cause the widest destabilisation of the community. When the IRA tried to murder the principal of Newry Model School in 1983 in front of a Primary 7 class, they were trying to murder someone who was also the clerk of session of Downshire Road Presbyterian Church. When the IRA killed Senator John Barnhill, they killed the clerk of session of Leckpatrick Presbyterian Church. Because of the deep sense of community within a Presbyterian congregation like that, to kill one person is to attack the community. Many people in a congregation will have relatives in the security forces. The IRA kill people, not uniforms.

The Reverend Roy Neill of First Castlederg Presbyterian Church has conducted the funerals of nine of his members who have been murdered by the IRA. The IRA have killed more than twenty people in that area: the repercussions of each murder were felt over a wide area. While relations between Protestants and Catholics have generally been good, the violence has aroused the old suspicions among Protestants, about who can be trusted. One IRA man blew himself up placing a bomb under the car of the man he went to work with every day. For all that, these particular Presbyterians are not precarious people, they are deeply rooted in that community. The IRA has not managed to move them from their homes and their farms; in other border areas, however, Protestants have been forced to move.

Perhaps what has been hardest to bear is a widespread sense that outside these grieving families, communities and Churches, few people seemed to care. The deep-seated feeling within the Presbyterian community is that the outside world, even that outside world no further away than Britain, never cared, for they mostly never knew or didn't want to know.

It is difficult to report grief in such a way that it can be understood by people who are not grieving. It would have been useful to deploy resources and televisual skill to reconstruct the planning and logistics behind the killing of some Protestants on isolated farms. That might have communicated the sense of threat under which many people lived. There was no shortage of material, for it happened often enough.

In ways which can only be experienced from within a community, carrying as it does its tribal nightmares, it is difficult to imagine how every murder shook the Protestant community like a tremor, particulary those communities in isolated areas around the border. The same can clearly be said about the effect of loyalist killings on, say, the Catholics of north Belfast.

Due to the threats posed by the IRA, it has been difficult for many members of the security forces to visit their families. I know of a Presbyterian minister who was considering moving to another congregation in Northern Ireland, in what, on the surface, would appear to be one of the most picturesque and lovely places in the country. His son, who is a police officer, was told that if his parents moved it would be too dangerous for him to visit them, as there was an active IRA unit with a support network operating in the area.

When I visit members of the congregation with children in the security forces, it is with lowered voice that the information is conveyed to me, and almost invariably they say that they don't usually tell people about it, and I am not to tell anyone else in case it would get back to the IRA and their son or daughter would be put at risk.

The result of all of this has been a significant shift of the Protestant population from the city of Belfast to the satellite towns, and a general movement from many border areas towards the heartlands of Presbyterianism.

HOW ARE WE TO REMEMBER?

All successfully travelled journeys of grief involve remembering, grieving and hoping. The only way to avoid the possibility of grief is to avoid the opportunities to love.

It is not possible for individuals to draw a line under their loss and get on with life as if nothing has happened. It would be callous for a community to travel into the future and leave grieving people behind.

Some people talk as if the violence of the last twenty-five years were inevitable. They seem to be saying that people had to get it out of their systems; things had to run their course. It is as if no one is morally responsible for what happened. If it is like that, then we cannot speak about forgiveness, because forgiveness presumes that someone or some people did something for which they are responsible and for which forgiveness might be appropriate. Forgiveness presumes guilt which in turn presumes accountability.

If, on the other hand, no one is responsible for anything, then we draw a line under it and forget it. This is very different from remembering and forgiving. It is not open to Christians to proceed on the assumption that things could not have been different.

The Reverend Lesley Carroll, who ministers in a loyalist area of Belfast, welcomed the statement from the Combined Loyalist Military Command announcing the ceasefire on 13 October 1994:

> In all sincerity, we offer to the loved ones of all innocent victims over the last twenty-five years, abject and true remorse. No words of ours will compensate for all the intolerable suffering they have undergone during the conflict.[1]

Commenting on the situation brought about by the ceasefires, she wrote:

> There is no way forward unless we first of all hear how we have caused the other to suffer. There is no room for triumphalism in these days of fragile hope. There is no forgetting that not only have Loyalists suffered, they have also caused suffering . . .
>
> Such recognition of our own faults is indeed a good place to

begin. It is a good beginning because it echoes a renewed desire within Unionism for each to take responsibility for themselves and their actions. Apportioning blame simply lets us off the hook. Abdicating responsibility will only hold the process up.[2]

During the period of the Troubles, over 3,200 people have been killed while over 6,000 have died in road accidents. Each one has been associated with grief. What makes the difference is the intention behind the deaths. David Bolton, a qualified social worker, in his submission to the Forum for Peace and Reconciliation in Dublin Castle, said that

the impact on survivors and those who mourn is of greatest significance. It is not alone the fact that someone has been killed, but also the manner of their death that is significant . . . Death and injury, caused by human intention and action (what Weil calls *affliction*), brings with it complications and adds to the experience of victimisation of the one who suffers. For many, they have known multiple deaths and injuries, where the sorrows of one experience are overtaken by the next. So people who mourn or who nurse within them the disability and the pain of injury, experience their loss within the context of the violence.

The focus of our considerations should not be in attempting to forget the past, but in determining how we should remember the past. Forgetting would not be a positive position for the victims of violence. The absence of violence may accentuate the futility of it all.

In the words of *Irish Times* journalist Fintan O'Toole:

. . . too much forgetting is dangerous . . . The real peacemaking which is to come demands generosity, commitment and fierce determination to defeat the zealots and bigots.

Those qualities will be inspired by remembering, not by forgetting, by turning away in horror and disgust, not by slumping into passive relief that the nightmare is over.

One of the functions of Remembrance Day services is to provide an opportunity for people to remember horrendous losses in silence. The most moving rituals are those which are accompanied by few words. These occasions enable people to come together, not primarily to be angry, but to remember. It reminds bereaved people that the loss of the people they love has not been forgotten.

One of the things that has kept Northern Ireland from descending into total chaos has been the willingness of some bereaved people to forgive those who killed the people they love, and the stated desire of them, and of many others, that there should be no revenge. One could imagine the way passions would have been aroused had these people done otherwise and given utterance to the anger they must often have felt.

Forgiveness is not easy. It is not simply a case of pressing a 'delete' key which, without cost, wipes out the past.

On the fiftieth anniversary of the liberation of Auschwitz in January 1995, the Nobel Prize winner and survivor of Auschwitz, Elie Wiesel, prayed:

> Although we know that God is merciful, please God do not have mercy on those who have created this place. God of forgiveness do not forgive those murderers of Jewish children . . . remember the nocturnal processions of children and more children and more children, frightened, quiet so quiet and so beautiful . . . God, merciful God, do not have mercy on those who had no mercy on Jewish children.[3]

Those words stopped me in my tracks. They focused my mind on the enormity of what had happened in the camps. Sometimes we seem to use the word forgiveness too glibly: forgiveness takes sin seriously.

There is no correspondence in scale between Auschwitz and Northern Ireland: the correspondence lies in the difficulty of forgiveness. It is not easy. The very possibility of forgiveness cost God the price of Christ's death. It is from that agony that the generosity of God's forgiveness proceeds. It is that which opens up a new future without denying the reality of the past.

For some, the long journey to forgiveness has been hard. Maura Kiely's journey is eloquently told in the book *Profiles of Hope*. Her son was shot by loyalists as he left St Bridget's Church in Belfast on the evening of 9 February 1975.

> I nearly lost my faith . . . At one point I began to think that there was no God. The week after the funeral I remember making a cup of coffee and suddenly throwing it over a picture of Our Lord . . . When I decided that the bitterness would have to go, something inside me kept saying, 'Go and meet someone else who has lost a son.' . . . It's amazing. When I look back now . . . out of evil comes good.[4]

Out of that experience came the Cross Group, for others who have lost a husband or a son or a relative as a result of violence.

Some have found or been given the resources to forgive. It may be that for them some of the bitterness abates more quickly than would be the case if they had found it impossible to forgive. Gordon and Joan Wilson's witness, not only challenges what goes on in this society, it keeps the memory of their daughter before people. She is not forgotten.

It is important to keep alive the memory of those who have died, and with it our determination that we will not let this happen ever again.

I have tried in this book to tell a story from within the perspective of the Presbyterian community but I readily acknowledge that it is not the only story.

It is important for Protestants to remember that loyalist paramilitaries killed over nine hundred people. That represents suffering and grief of monumental proportions, imposed upon the Catholic community. Along with that went fear, for terrorism involves naked terror. The news reports have recorded funeral after funeral from Catholic churches. Every death has left behind a close network of grieving people. However much Protestants may feel the pain of republican violence, we need to remember that the suffering has not all been on one side. It is not only Protestant families which have been left desolate.

On top of the statistics of death are the physical and mental injuries of those who survived, but who will never again have sight, or limbs, or normal mobility. For some of them there is constant pain. In some cases members of the family have had to give up jobs and become carers.

One of the most moving services I was ever involved in was connected with the Disabled Police Officers' Association broadcast from Rosemary Church by Ulster Television on 7 November 1993. Some of those officers will spend the rest of their lives in wheelchairs; others have lost their sight and some their arms and hands. I found that service a profoundly moving experience, not least because it demonstrated the capacity of many seriously injured people not to be destroyed by what had happened to them. Their determination to cope with the consequences of their injuries was marked by remarkable faith and even cheerfulness. The courage and faith of those people was very evident.

If it is the case that at least 10 people have been very closely associated with each of the over 3,200 people who have been killed, there are 32,000 traumatised people. When the 37,000 who have been injured are added to that, along with those who have seen their premises destroyed, we are talking about a mountain of memories. How are we going to deal with all of this? It can't all be deleted from the collective memory.

To keep the memories alive so that they fester will only disable us for the future. We could remember with carefully nurtured bitterness, which would do more damage to the bereaved than to the guilty. We could remember in a negative way which would guarantee that the past would control the future. Stories can be conduits of distress for generations.

There is a deep well of compassion in the heart of God and infinite resources of grace. On the cross God suffered and spoke remarkable words of forgiveness. The Resurrection broke the iron connection between the past and the future and Pentecost brought 'joy beyond sorrow and beauty beyond horror'.

DIVERSITY AND FREEDOM

LIMITING BELIEFS

Seamus Heaney, in an interview in *The Times* in 1984, spoke of the tension between the individual and the group in Ireland:

> Everyone in the North is born with a sense of solidarity with one or the other group. So the emergent self grows, carrying responsibility for the group, holding the line, keeping up the side. But as you come to different awarenesses you know that there are complicated concessions to be made; truths to be told beyond the official shibboleths . . . and yet the moment you set them down . . . it seems like betrayals . . . you become conscious that you are not just yourself, you are part of the group . . . so the idea of the freed self becomes very attractive.

This book has been written from a Presbyterian perspective; not, hopefully, totally uncritical of the community out of which it comes. There is a story to be told, but there are also truths to be told beyond the official shibboleths and there are complicated concessions to be made.

Seamus Heaney wrote in *Station Island*:

> I hate how quick I was to know my place.
> I hate where I was born, hate everything
> that made me biddable and unforthcoming.[1]

A system which makes people biddable and unforthcoming does not provide them with freedom. It invites resistance. We owe it to one another to have some kind of vision which goes beyond the protection of our own group to the liberation of the other. To fail to do that is to remain in the ideological prison, for imprisonment requires prison officers as well as prisoners.

Dr S.C. Papenfus in an unpublished paper on 'Assumptions: a psychology of governing beliefs' draws attention to two kinds of beliefs that people may have:

> 'Limiting beliefs', which are expressed in a sense of dread, which is a combination of 'expectation and fear', lead us to be defensive and self-protective. The psychological traps that are associated with these 'limiting beliefs' are guilt, shame, self-pity, resentment and worry. Not having experienced unconditional love and forgiveness, such persons are condemning and hostile and resistant to change.
>
> On the other hand those who know of unconditional love are much more open to themselves and to other people, open to transformation, possessing a sense of inner freedom.

The Churches in Ireland, which are supposed to know about and to live out of an experience of the unconditional love of God, should be able to be open to themselves and to other people.

The historical experiences we have inflicted upon others and endured ourselves have schooled us in the 'limiting beliefs' marked by expectation and fear. The consequent political philosophies have been defensive and self-protective. Political and ecclesiastical institutions which carry the inherited fearful expectations of the wider community can be destructive of the work of the Spirit, the fruit of whose work is 'love and joy, and peace and gentleness'.

The strict beat of conformity, along with 'the dwelling on days gone by and the brooding over past history' destroys the expectation that God might yet do new things (Isaiah 43:18 and 19).

The temptation is to collude with this spirit of brooding over the past in order to survive; but is it survival or death? The preaching of the gospel contains an invitation to be open to an unexpected future which is no more determined by the past than the possibility of the Resurrection was closed down by the Crucifixion.

The siege of Derry and the Battle of the Boyne continue as powerful symbols from the past, as well as interpretive models of the present, because they speak about the periodic threat of being overwhelmed by a majority. We could do with some alternative interpretive models.

Where does the passionate energy come from which erupts into violence? It lurks within the sectarianism of this society. It incarnates itself in the principalities and powers of ideological, political and ecclesiastical structures and keeps a people, who are supposed to be liberated, employed as anxious defenders. They thereby create the very conditions of alienation and mis-understanding which nurture the things they most fear. This mentality has had spiritual and cultural implications as well as political. We are a people who live behind spiritual, political and ecclesiastical ramparts. We behave like batsmen facing hostile fast bowling on an uneven pitch: more concerned to survive than to win the match; playing for a draw at best; always defensive; seldom taking the initiative.

While all of this may be historically understandable, it has not served us well in the last twenty-five years.

The recurring political opportunities since 1968 have required new, but necessary, attitudes of understanding, imagination, generosity and determination as well as a willingness to develop trust across ancient lines of rupture. Having failed seriously and consistently to achieve this, the situation of the Protestant community deteriorates.

Such qualities do not come from a mentality rooted in the ideological construct of siege, but they can be nurtured by people who have themselves been nurtured by the unmerited and generous grace of God. We can no longer afford defensive, self-defeating ways of thinking.

OPERATIVE VALUES

Marianne Elliott wrote:

> ... although the state of Northern Ireland, with the old fears of encirclement inbuilt, has more often than not presented the more conservative side of the Protestant ethos, the libertarian tradition is still active in the anti-authoritarian tendency which causes Protestants to band together in assertion of their own brand of direct democracy against feared 'sell-outs' by politicians who take no account of their special status within the governing process. To dig one's heels in and rest one's case on antiquity may appear reactionary; in Presbyterian terms it is continuation of that radical tradition of resisting an authority which has betrayed its trust ... This belief in liberty of conscience and the primacy of the individual is still reflected in Presbyterianism's democratic church structure.[2]

Is it possible for a people with a defensive siege mentality to articulate a political vision which provides honour and space for everyone?

Peter Berger and Richard Neuhaus maintained that the Christian Church

> is a primary agent for bearing and transmitting the operative values for our society ... In the absence of the church and other mediating structures that articulate these values, the result is not that the society is left without operative values; the result is that the state has an unchallenged monopoly on the generation and maintenance of values.[3]

If these issues are not addressed in preaching, and if the Kingdom values of love, forgiveness, repentance, righteousness and reconciliation, and the rights which people have by virtue of being made in God's image, and the duties which they must fulfil since they were bought, not with silver or gold, but with the precious blood of Jesus Christ, are not brought before congregations, it will hardly be surprising if the people who constitute the Church hold opinions which are no different from those who never come.

Those who claim that they speak in the name of God, which is what Presbyterians do, must not forget that God causes the sun to shine and the rain to fall on all kinds of people. It is the task of any Church which names the name of God to have concerns beyond the interests of its own members. While it may be necessary from time to time to be primarily concerned with a defence of their legitimate interests, that must not translate itself into a selfish and unending defence of their interests alone.

I hope that Presbyterians reading this story have felt that at least a part of their story has been told. It is necessary for us in turn to listen to the other stories.

I hope that those who have read it who are not Presbyterians will have read something which has increased their understanding, even if they have not agreed with all that I have written.

At the end of the day, knowing people involves meeting people and since many of us live in homogeneous communities where we meet largely like-minded people, we need to make some conscious efforts to break out of those isolated communities. Any minister who is going to preach the truth of the gospel in Ireland needs to know about some of the experiences which people have had on the other side of divisions in Ireland. To know requires a willingness to cross some of those frontiers.

Preparation for preaching the Word of God, for 'bearing and transmitting the operative values of our society' will involve study, prayer and reflection, but, in addition, it will involve personal, and perhaps unsettling, journeys across frontiers. Some of the longest emotional journeys in Ireland are, in fact, quite short geographically. It means leaving largely self-sufficient and powerful ecclesiastical institutions on journeys of faith, down the road.

Campbell Moreland, a young Belfast doctor diagnosed as having cancer, wrote of his experience:

> An analogy to living with cancer is solitary confinement: once inside the prison you are trapped; you can walk around, examine the furniture, scrutinise the walls until you know every crack in the plaster, and look out the window . . . The most useful people and the best doctors are those prepared to come inside the cell, sit down, and spend some time with you. The outsider can then adjust his or her horizon to that of the patient and will be able to see the cell much as the patient sees it, although never quite the same. A person of no help to the patient is the one who opens the hatch on the door and says, 'I can see your cell, its furniture, the cracks in the wall, but I am not coming in. Here are some books, have an injection, things will soon be all right, and you will be able to come out', closes the hatch and disappears.[4]

In Ireland, the two communities, and the Churches associated with them, are in two such cells. What is required is not confrontational theology and manipulative, duplicitous politics, but service by each Church to the other. There is not going to be peace in Ireland which is not the fruit of understanding.

The powerful seldom know how powerful they really are. It is as we listen to other people that we appreciate the agony of suffering which is not physical, but the psychic oppression of not being noticed or valued for one's own sake.

As I listen to some women speak about their experience of the Church, I am aware of them saying that some preachers, as significant figures within the Church, are so insensitive to them that in order to survive they have to co-exist with the Church. They can't move closer without being in danger of being destroyed by an institution which presses down upon them. It's not done deliberately of course, at least not usually.

There is much unconscious 'bearing down' upon one another in Ireland and it has not been alleviated by very much sensitive listening. The Catholic majority in Ireland bears down on the Protestant minority; the Protestant majority in the north bears down on the Catholic minority; the British (or English) bear down on both!

In Acts 10 we are given the breakthrough story of the Jewish Christian, Peter, communicating the gospel to the Gentile Cornelius. Peter refused to let Cornelius kneel in front of him. 'Stand up,' said Peter; 'I myself am only a man.' The good news was communicated with both of them standing.

It is possible to be orthodox in all kinds of ways but still be reinforcing the strongholds of racism. John Perkins, a black North American and evangelical from Mississippi, has expressed it like this:

> Black and white churches alike have so moulded their message to fit within cultural, racial and religious traditions, that they have robbed the gospel of its power. It was powerless to reach across racial, cultural, economic and social barriers.[5]

Might this not also be said about our Churches in Ireland? Theologically and evangelically Presbyterian, ecclesiologically impeccably Roman, exquisitely liturgically Anglican, warm-heartedly Methodist, but essentially providing the ordinances of religion to imprisoned people?

It is entirely possible to be ministers or priests in strong and enthusiastic congregations, which provide people with a sense of identity and belonging, which, in so far as they are exclusive and excluding communities, are in fact counter-signs against the values of the Kingdom of God.

Whatever kind of dreams we may have about the future of this country, they will have to be sufficiently accommodating to honour and protect the particularities of diverse people.

> The identities of the communities within this island are such that minorities are not going to permit themselves to be discriminated against or swallowed up without remainder by any of the majorities. It thus follows that we must work with models of co-operation and not with models of domination or assimilation.

Within the whole island, the significance of the culture, religion and identity of the Protestant minority must be recognised, honoured and protected.

Within Northern Ireland the significance of the culture, religion and identity of the Roman Catholic minority must be recognised, honoured and protected . . .

Can we then in our self-consciousness begin to hold our particular identities within larger communities? If we are to diminish the negative elements in the socialisation processes we need the help of our neighbours to overcome our suspicions and anxieties.

Unionists need to know that they are recognised and honoured by Nationalists. This is a responsibility which devolves upon Nationalists. Unionists cannot do this for themselves. This means that Nationalists in both parts of the island need to be heard and seen to be concerned about the wellbeing of Unionists as well as Nationalists. This is not the case at present.

Nationalists need to know that they are recognised and honoured by Unionists. This is a responsibility which devolves upon Unionists. Nationalists cannot do this for themselves. This means that Unionists in both parts of the island need to be heard and seen to be concerned about the wellbeing of Nationalists as well as Protestants. This is not the case at present.[6]

A CHANGING IRELAND

Ireland is changing. I indicated the fear which Protestants have that Catholic social teaching can be imposed on an unwilling Protestant minority. The likelihood of this kind of imposition happening in Ireland is receding.

Dr Gordon Graham argues that

the power of the [Catholic] church to influence social policy and political events is seriously limited by the freedoms liberal democracy has established . . . there is in reality nothing to be feared from an aspiration and self-understanding which, in the modern world, cannot be realized.[7]

We are living in a changing Ireland to which Protestants need to respond in a creative way. I see three areas of change.

Firstly, Irish Catholicism is changing. It is becoming more open and more friendly to Presbyterians than vice versa. The hand of friendship is reached out to us more often than it is extended in reverse. Ecumenism has made of Protestants separated brothers and sisters, rather than strangers and aliens. For many Catholics, a Presbyterian church is not any longer a place to be shunned at all costs. No longer do Catholics stand outside a Protestant church for a funeral. Without denying the unresolved differences which still exist between us, we must do all we can to build ties of friendship and co-operation.

Secondly, Irish Catholic nationalism is taking the majority community in Northern Ireland more seriously than before. The Downing Street Declaration left Britain in a politically attached but ideologically semi-detached position from Northern Ireland, not unlike that of a wife saying to her husband, 'You can stay here as long as you like, but any time you want to go and live with someone else, I will facilitate your departure'. That is an unsettling situation.

The designs which the Republic has on the 'fourth green field' have been moderated so that the fulfilment of their dream of a united Ireland can only come about when a majority of people in Northern Ireland share the same dream, which is unlikely in the foreseeable future. The Declaration has nevertheless moved the political centre of gravity in this direction.

Now that some of the pressure has been removed and consent acknowledged as including the right to say 'No', it is imperative that we build as many constructive relationships as we can. However east–west the orientation of some Presbyterians may be, there are a significant number of our Catholic neighbours who live with a practical, emotional and ideological north–south orientation which needs to be respected.

The third change is the cessation of paramilitary violence.

Hopefully, the recurring nightmare of republican and loyalist violence will not rip through the night air ever again.

It is above all necessary that we be pro-active in whatever way we can in building confidence across these ancient lines of rupture. In a situation where violence has ended and relationships of confidence and trust are being established, we may be able to address, promote and defend issues of justice without first screening them through lenses of political bias.

Christians in Ireland are a people who believe in the Trinity. Jürgen Moltmann suggested the implications which this has for the ordering of society:

> ... the Trinity corresponds to a community in which people are defined in their relations with one another and in their significance for one another, not in opposition to one another, in terms of power and possession ... The doctrine of the Trinity constitutes the church as 'a community free of dominion'. The trinitarian principle replaces the principle of power by the principle of concord ... I am free and feel myself to be truly free when I am respected and recognised by others and when I for my part respect and recognise them ... Then the other person is no longer the limitation of my freedom; he is an expansion of it.[8]

THE CONCLUSION

The 1992 'Mission Statement' received by the General Assembly at its meeting to mark the 350th anniversary of the first presbytery in Ireland declares:

> The Presbyterian Church in Ireland
> as a Reformed Church within the wider body of Christ
> is grounded in the Scriptures,
> and exists to love and honour God
> through faith in his Son and by the power of the His Spirit,
> and to enable her members to play their part
> in fulfilling God's mission to our world.

God calls us to a shared life
in which we love, honour and are reconciled to one another
whilst respecting our diversity
within the Presbyterian Church in Ireland.
We are called to encourage
the exercise of the gifts of every member of the Body
for the work of ministry and,
seeking the renewal of the whole Church,
to co-operate with other parts of Christ's Church
without betrayal of our convictions.

God calls us to worship Him with our whole lives,
meeting together in groups large and small
and gathering especially on the Lord's Day
for the preaching and study of His word,
the celebration of the sacraments
and the offering of prayer and praise with reverence and joy,
using language, form and music appropriate
both to Scripture and to our time and culture.

God calls us to mission as witnesses to Christ
through both evangelism and social witness
challenging the values of the world in which we live
with the values of God's kingdom
and winning men and women to faith and discipleship.
This mission is to be pursued amongst all the people of Ireland
and the peoples of the European Community and the whole
    world:
those with whom we feel comfortable,
those from whom we feel alienated
and those who are in any way distant from us in culture and
    faith.

We ourselves are challenged with a biblical discipleship which is
    radical
in its self denial,
simplicity of lifestyle,
stewardship of money,
faithful relationships,

prayerfulness,
concern for the world which God has created
and love for its people whom He loves
and for whose salvation He gave His Son.[9]

The Presbyterian Church in Ireland cannot at the end of the day avoid the consequences of its own name. It is a Presbyterian Church, and not a sect. Its members live in both the United Kingdom and in Ireland. It is set among the people of Ireland. It needs to come to terms in a positive way with all that is involved in its name, whatever the political arrangements happen to be. As long as we fail to do this, we will live in a confused world feeling only partly at home, amongst a people with whom we have not yet made peace, while at the same time having no other place to go which would be more congenial.

Or do we suspect that here we have no abiding city and that the Plantation will yet be reversed and we will, however reluctantly, return to the place whence we came 350 years ago, and Ireland shall know us no more?

If we are intending to stay, let us do so in peace, seeking necessary space for ourselves and giving the same necessary space to others, who do not like being pushed around any more than we do.

NOTES

CHAPTER 1

1 The statistics which are for 1993 are taken from the *Irish Christian Handbook 1995/96*, edited by Peter Brierley and Boyd Myers, Christian Research, 1994, pp. 34, 36, 44

2 Church and Government Committee's submission to Initiative '92 (not published). See *A Citizens' Inquiry: The Opsahl Report on Northern Ireland*, edited by Andy Pollak, Lilliput Press, 1993, pp. 102, 130, 358

3 Stewart, A.T.Q. *The Narrow Ground*, Faber and Faber, 1977, p. 83

4 Davey, J. Ernest. 'A survey of our past as a Church' in *Three Hundred Years of Presbyterianism: Sermon and Addresses*, Tercentenary Committee of the Presbyterian Church in Ireland, 1943, pp. 19–20

5 Lee, J.J. *Ireland 1912–1985*, Cambridge University Press 1989, pp. 3–4

6 *Code of the Presbyterian Church in Ireland*, Church House Belfast, 1980, revised 1992, p. 10

7 Fulton, Austin. *J. Ernest Davey, The Presbyterian Church in Ireland*, 1970, pp. 31, 97

8 General Assembly Minutes, 1980, p. 55

9 *The Shorter Catechism*, question 1

10 'Presbyterian principles and political witness in Northern Ireland', General Assembly Annual Reports, 1993

CHAPTER 2

1 Loughrey, Patrick (ed.). *The People of Ireland*, Appletree Press, 1988, pp. 38–9

2 *Ibid.*, p. 44

3 Bardon, Jonathan. *A History of Ulster*, Blackstaff Press, 1992, pp. 131, 132

4 *Ibid.*, p. 128

5 *Ibid.*, p. 137

6 *Ibid.*, p. 139

7 Kennedy, Alistair. 'Church planting in Irish Presbyterianism, 1600–1992', a series of articles published in monthly issues of *Presbyterian Herald* between November 1992–April 1993

8 Fitzpatrick, Rory. *God's Frontiersmen: The Scots-Irish Epic*, Weidenfeld and Nicolson, 1989, p. 16

9 Reid, James Seaton. *History of the Presbyterian Church in Ireland*, William Mullan, 1867, p. 106

10 Bardon, Jonathan. *A History of Ulster*, Blackstaff Press, 1992, p. 171

11 *Ibid.*

12 Marshall, R.L. 'The commemoration sermon' in *Three Hundred Years of Presbyterianism: Sermon and Addresses*, Tercentenary Committee of the Presbyterian Church in Ireland, 1943, pp. 7, 9

13 Kennedy, Alistair. 'Church planting in Irish Presbyterianism, 1660–1992', a series of articles published in monthly issues of *Presbyterian Herald* between November 1992–April 1993

14 Holmes, Finlay. *Henry Cooke*, Christian Journals, 1981, pp. 47–76

15 Davey, J. Ernest. *1840–1940: The Story of a Hundred Years*, W. & G. Baird, 1940, p. 10

16 Holmes, R.F.G. *Our Irish Presbyterian Heritage*, Publications Committee of the Presbyterian

Church in Ireland, 1985, and
Holmes, Finlay. *Henry Cooke,*
Christian Journals, 1981. The
subscription controversy is dealt
with in detail in *Challenge and
Conflict: Essays in Irish
Presbyterian History and Doctrine,*
W. & G. Baird, 1981
17 Burleigh, J.H.S. *A Church History
of Scotland,* Oxford University
Press, 1960, pp. 352–3

CHAPTER 3

1 The statistics which are for 1993
are taken from the *Irish Christian
Handbook 1995/96,* edited by
Peter Brierley and Boyd Myers,
Christian Research, 1994, p. 36
2 Hebblethwaite, Peter. *The Year of
Three Popes,* Collins/Fount, 1978,
pp. 95–6
3 Barbour, Noel. 'Impotent or
powerful? The Catholic Church
in Ireland', editorial, *Studies,*
vol. 83, no. 332 (winter 1994)
4 Dunn, Joseph. *No Lions in the
Hierarchy: An Anthology of Sorts,*
Columba Press, 1994
5 FitzGerald, Garret. *All in a Life,*
Gill and Macmillan, 1991,
pp. 184–5
6 The Pontifical Council for
Promoting Christian Unity,
Vatican City, Information
Service: N. 74 1990 (III)
7 General Assembly Annual
Reports, 1990, p. 23
8 Meeking, Basil and John Stott
(eds). *The Evangelical–Roman
Catholic Dialogue on Mission,
1977–84: A Report,* William B.
Eerdmans and Paternoster Press,
1986
9 O Connor, Fionnuala. *In Search
of a State: Catholics in Northern
Ireland,* Blackstaff Press, 1993
10 'The report of the working party
on sectarianism: a discussion
document for presentation to the
Irish Inter-church Meeting',

1993, p. 23. Available from 48
Elmwood Avenue, Belfast 9

CHAPTER 4

1 McNeill, Mary. *The Life and
Times of Mary Ann McCracken,
1770–1866: A Belfast Panorama,*
Blackstaff Press, 1988, p. 189
2 Kernohan, J.W. *Rosemary Street
Presbyterian Church, Belfast: A
Record of the Past 200 Years,*
'Witness' Office, 1923
3 Marshall, W.F. *Ulster Sails West,*
bi-centennial edition, Century
Services, 1976
4 Cromie, Howard. *Ulster Settlers
in America,* Irish Mission
Publications, 1984, p. 10
5 Bardon, Jonathan. *A History of
Ulster,* Blackstaff Press, 1992,
p. 217
6 Some of the material in this
chapter appears in the author's
'The self-understanding of
Protestants in Northern Ireland'
in *Irish Challenges to Theology,*
edited by Enda McDonagh,
Dominican Publications, 1986,
pp. 5–20
7 Hannan, Mark. 'A kingdom of
justice', *Racial Justice,* (summer
1985), p. 4
8 Stewart, A.T.Q. *The Narrow
Ground,* Faber and Faber, 1977,
p. 108
9 Holmes, Finlay. *Henry Cooke,*
Christian Journals, 1981, pp. 64,
65–6
10 Bardon, Jonathan. *A History of
Ulster,* Blackstaff Press, 1992,
pp. 367, 370
11 Holmes, R.F.G. *Our Irish
Presbyterian Heritage,* Publications
Committee of the Presbyterian
Church in Ireland, 1985, p. 130
12 Armour, W.S. *Armour of
Ballymoney,* Duckworth, 1934
13 McMinn, J.R.B. 'Against the
tide: A calendar of the papers of
Rev J B Armour, Irish

Presbyterian minister and Home Ruler, 1869–1914', PRONI, 1985, p. lx. Quoted by kind permission of the Deputy Keeper of the Records, PRONI.

14 Bowen, D. *Paul, Cardinal Cullen and the Shaping of Modern Irish Catholicism*, Gill and Macmillan, 1983, p. 106

15 Holmes, Finlay. 'The nineteenth century: the battle for the soul of Ireland', *Christian Irishman* (June 1984), p. 16

16 McCaughey, Terence P. *Memory and Redemption: Church, Politics and Prophetic Theology in Ireland*, Gill and Macmillan, 1993, p. 35

17 General Assembly Minutes, 1912

18 For a fuller discussion see Helmick, Raymond, 'Church structure and violence in Northern Ireland', *The Month*, August 1977, p. 273

19 Heaney, Seamus. 'Correspondences: emigrations and inner exiles' in *Migrations: The Irish at Home and Abroad*, edited by Richard Kearney, Wolfhound Press, 1990, p. 27

20 O'Brien, Conor Cruise. *Ancestral Voices: Religion and Nationalism in Ireland*, Poolbeg, 1994, p. 139

21 Holmes, R.F.G. *Our Irish Presbyterian Heritage*, Publications Committee of the Presbyterian Church in Ireland, 1985, pp. 147–8

22 Irish Episcopal Conference submission to the New Ireland Forum, January 1984, Veritas Publications, 1984, pp. 3, 20

23 Harris, Mary. *The Catholic Church and the Establishment of Northern Ireland*, Cork University Press, 1994

24 *Abortion and the Right to Life*, CTS, 1980, quoted by John Haldane (Centre for Philosophy and Public Affairs, University of St Andrews) in 'Catholic social

teaching and communitarianism' at a conference in Queen's University Belfast on 'Religious identity and political community', 19 November 1992

25 McCann, Eamonn. *War and an Irish Town*, Pluto Press, 1980, pp. 12–13

26 Fulton, Austin. *J. Ernest Davey, The Presbyterian Church in Ireland*, 1970, p. 43

27 General Assembly Annual Reports, 1967, p. 121

28 Bardon, Jonathan. *A History of Ulster*, Blackstaff Press, 1992, p. 631

29 Cameron Report. *Disturbances in Northern Ireland: Report of the Commission Appointed by the Governor of Northern Ireland*, HMSO, Cmd 532, 1969

30 General Assembly Annual Reports, 1993, p. 14

31 Report of the Presbyterian Church USA Committee on Mission Responsibility Through Investment, 1987, p. 3, 4

32 General Assembly Annual Reports, 1994, p. 5

CHAPTER 5

1 Davey, J. Ernest. 'A survey of our past as a Church' in *Three Hundred Years of Presbyterianism: Sermon and Addresses*, Tercentenary Committee of the Presbyterian Church in Ireland, 1943, p. 12

2 Holmes, Finlay. 'The penalties of non-conformity in seventeenth-century Ireland', *Christian Irishman* (January 1984), p. 11

3 Bardon, Jonathan. *A History of Ulster*, Blackstaff Press, 1992, p. 176

4 Kennedy, Alistair. 'Church planting in Irish Presbyterianism, 1600–1992', a

series of articles published in monthly issues of *Presbyterian Herald* between November 1992–April 1993

5 Akenson, Donald Harman. *The Irish Diaspora*, Institute of Irish Studies, Queen's University Belfast, 1993, p. 29

6 Barkley, John M. *Blackmouth & Dissenter*, White Row Press, 1991, p. 153

7 Baskin, Bibi. *Protestants in a Catholic State*, documentary on RTE/UTV, 1991

8 Holmes, R.F.G. *Our Irish Presbyterian Heritage*, Publications Committee of the Presbyterian Church in Ireland, 1985, p. 145

9 General Assembly Minutes, 1994, p. 250

10 Stevens, David. 'Protestants in the Republic' in *Culture in Ireland – Division or Diversity?*, edited by Edna Longley, Institute of Irish Studies, Queen's University Belfast, 1991, pp. 144, 145

11 Griffin, Dean. *Protestants in a Catholic State*, documentary on RTE/UTV, 1991

12 Butler, Herbert. *Protestants in a Catholic State*, documentary on RTE/UTV, 1991

13 Sweeney, Paul. An address printed by the Northern Ireland Voluntary Trust in 1991

14 Adapted from 'The siege mentality', John Dunlop, *Presbyterian Herald* (June 1991), pp. 10–11

CHAPTER 6

1 Stewart, David. *The Seceders in Ireland, with Annals of their Congregations*, Presbyterian Historical Society, 1950, p. 39

2 Gonzalez, Justo (ed.). *Proclaiming the Acceptable Year*, Judson Press, 1982, pp. 10–11,

reprinted by permission of the publisher, Judson Press, 1-800-458-3766

3 Quinlan, Seán. 'The olive tree in the Forum', *Furrow*, vol. 33, no. 1 (January 1982), p. 3

4 *The Shorter Catechism*, question 14

5 Hewitt, John. 'An Irishman in Coventry', *The Collected Poems of John Hewitt*, edited by Frank Ormsby, Blackstaff Press, 1991, p. 97

6 *The Shorter Catechism*, question 4

7 Burleigh, J.H.S. *A Church History of Scotland*, Oxford University Press, 1960, pp. 307–8, regarding the impression made upon the young Thomas Chalmers by Professor George Hill

8 General Assembly Annual Reports, 1992, p. 89

9 Viviers, Gerardo. Review in *Transformation*, vol. 1, no. 2 (April/June 1984), p. 29. See *Protestantism and Repression*, Rubem Alves, SCM Press, 1985

10 Conn, Harvie M. 'Sin in the city: the privatization myth', *Occasional Essays*, Latin American Evangelical Center for Pastoral Studies (June 1984), p. 33, quoting from David Claerbout, *Urban Ministry*, Zondervan, 1983

CHAPTER 7

1 *Westminster Confession of Faith*, chapter XXVIII:1

2 Rodgers, W.R. 'Epilogue to the Character of Ireland', *Poems*, Gallery Press, 1993. Quoted by kind permission of The Gallery Press

3 *Belfast Telegraph*, 5 January 1995

4 Waters, John. *Irish Times*, 24 January 1995

5 O'Faolain, Nuala. *Irish Times*, Christmas 1992

6   Dunlop, John, *Thought for the Day*, BBC Radio 4, 10 September 1994
7   McCaughey, Terence P. *Memory and Redemption: Church, Politics and Prophetic Theology in Ireland*, Gill and Macmillan, 1993, p. 53

CHAPTER 8

1   Cairns, Ed. *Caught in Crossfire: Children and the Northern Ireland Conflict*, Appletree Press, 1987, pp. 95, 104
2   Heaney, Seamus. 'Correspondences: emigrations and inner exiles' in *Migrations: The Irish at Home and Abroad*, edited by Richard Kearney, Wolfhound Press, 1990, pp. 22, 23
3   Stevens, David. 'Protestants in the Republic' in *Culture in Ireland – Division or Diversity?*, edited by Edna Longley, Institute of Irish Studies, Queen's University Belfast, 1991, pp. 142, 143
4   General Assembly Annual Reports, 1988, p. 330; General Assembly Minutes, 1988, p. 54
5   From 'The message of the mission', a lecture by R.J. Rodgers delivered at the Presbyterian Historical Society on 22 November 1990; printed in *The Bulletin of the Presbyterian Historical Society of Ireland*, vol. 20 (March 1991), and subsequently in *Christian Irishman* (November 1991), p. 28
6   Clarke, Austin. 'Burial of an Irish president' in *Poetry after Yeats: Seven Poets*, edited by Maurice Harmon, Wolfhound Press, 1979, p. 46

CHAPTER 9

1   Lee, Simon. 'Province's future', *Irish Times*, 14 October 1993
2   Brown, Terence. 'British Ireland' in *Culture in Ireland – Division or Diversity?*, edited by Edna Longley, Institute of Irish Studies, Queen's University Belfast, 1991, pp. 73–4, 75
3   Some of what follows is contained in an article written for *Doctrine and Life*, vol. 43 (November 1993), being the published version of a lecture ('Questioning the ideologies') given at the 30th Glenstal Ecumenical Conference in July 1993. The conference theme was 'The awkward voice: prophecy today'.
4   Available on four cassette tapes from Princeton Theological Seminary, Princeton NJ 08542, USA

CHAPTER 10

1   Statement from Combined Loyalist Military Command as printed in *Belfast Telegraph*, 13 October 1994
2   Carroll, Lesley. *The Month*, vol. 27, no. 11 (November 1994)
3   *Independent*, London, 27 January 1995
4   Maura Kiely quoted in *Profiles of Hope*, Alf McCreary, Christian Journals, 1981, p. 44, 45, 47

CHAPTER 11

1   Heaney, Seamus. *Station Island*, Faber and Faber, 1984, p. 85
2   Elliott, Marianne. *Watchmen in Sion: The Protestant Idea of Liberty*, Field Day Pamphlet No. 8, 1983, pp. 27 and 8
3   Berger, Peter and Richard Neuhaus, *To Empower People: The*

Role of Mediating Structures in Public Policy, American Enterprise Institute for Public Policy Research, 1977, p. 30

4 Moreland, Campbell. *Lancet*, 24 July 1982, p. 203

5 Perkins, John. *Let Justice Roll Down: John Perkins Tells his own Story* (1976) and *With Justice for All* (1982), both published by Regal Books, a division of GL Publications

6 Church and Government Committee's submission to Initiative '92 (not published). See *A Citizens' Inquiry: The Opsahl Report on Northern Ireland*, edited by Andy Pollak, Lilliput Press, 1993, pp. 102, 130, 358

7 Graham, Gordon. Centre for Philosophy and Public Affairs, University of St Andrews, unpublished paper delivered at seminar on 'Religious identity and political community' in Queen's University Belfast, 19 November 1992

8 Moltmann, Jürgen. *The Trinity and the Kingdom of God: The Doctrine of God*, translated by Margaret Kohl, SCM Press, 1981, pp. 198, 202, 216

9 'Mission Statement', General Assembly Reports, 1992, pp. 89–90

INDEX

Alves, Rubem, 92
American War of Independence,
44–5
Anglican Church, 2, 23, 28, 43, 44,
139
and Presbyterians, 25–6, 46, 48,
110
and unionism, 49
Anglo-Irish Agreement, 99
Anglo-Irish relations, 100–1
Anglo-Irish War, 65
Anglo-Normans, 19
Antrim, County, 22, 46, 79–80
Antrim presbytery, 22
Armour, Reverend J.B., 48
art, 85
Associate Presbytery, 28
Atwood, Alex, 37–8, 43
Auschwitz, 129

Ballymena presbytery, 47
baptism, 95–6
Bardon, Jonathan, 21, 47
Barkley, Principal John M., 65, 67
Barnhill, Senator John, 125
Basic Code, 98–9
Belfast, 45, 56, 60, 68–9, 89
population shifts, 126
Presbyterians in, 78–9
sectarianism, 47
United Irishmen, 43–4, 46
beliefs, limiting, 133–6
Berger, Peter, 136
bibliolatry, 83
Blair, Robert, 22
Bolton, David, 1–2, 128
Bolton, Reverend Maurice, 72
Bowen, Desmond, 48–9
Boyne, Battle of the, 25, 135
British Army, 115
British Council of Churches, 16
Britishness, 115–16
Brown, Professor Terence, 107,
117–18
Brueggemann, Walter, 119–20
Bryce, James, 28
Bushmills, County Antrim, 23
Butler, Herbert, 72

Calvin, John, 18
Cameron Report, 56
Carey, Archbishop, 8
Carlisle Road, Derry, 73
Carrickfergus, County Antrim, 21, 64
Carroll, Reverend Lesley, 127–8
Casaroli, Archbishop, 35
Catholic Church, 2, 7, 23, 25, 31, 139
allegiance to, 99
changing, 141
church attendance, 8, 32
mixed marriages, 65–6
Presbyterian attitude to, 31–42,
111–13
in Republic, 50–4
sense of crisis, 33–4
social teaching, 52–3, 140
ultramontanism, 48–50
Catholic Emancipation, 47
Catholics, 43, 126
in Belfast, 79
culture of, 87, 94–7, 102
displaced, 22
identity of, 108–10
population shifts, 80–1
Cavan, County, 22
ceasefire (1994), 1, 102, 141–2
Celts, 19
Charles I, King, 63
Church of Scotland, 11, 22, 27, 28
Churches
agents for change, 136–40
ideological captivity, 119–21
civil rights movement, 56–7
Civil War, Irish, 65
Claerbout, David, 92
Clare, Dr Anthony, 74
Clarke, Austin, 113
Clonard Church, 33
colonisation, 103
Columbia Theological Seminary, 117
Combined Loyalist Military
Command, 127
communion, 89–90, 95, 96
community development, 87
Conference of European Churches,
16
Constitution, Irish, 53